Someday Homes Fill My Dreams

The Artwork and Poetry of
Emily Pittman

number three in the
Torbay Bight Press
Artists' Series

TORBAY BIGHT PRESS

Torbay
Newfoundland and Labrador

Published in Canada by

Torbay Bight Press

an imprint of Komatik Press

62 Lower Street, Torbay,

Newfoundland and Labrador,

A1K 1B3

www.komatikpress.com

rexkomatik@gmail.com

All images © 2017, 2018, 2019, 2020, 2021 by Emily Pittman

www.emilypittman.ca

ISBN (paperback) 978-1-950065-08-0

ISBN (hardcover) 978-1-950065-10-3

ISBN (eBook) 978-1-950065-12-7

Book design by

Rex Passion and Christina Parker

Cover design by Rex Passion

Torbay Bight Press is an imprint of Komatik Press

Torbay Bight Press
Artists' Series Introduction

In 2019, we created the Torbay Bight Press *Artists' Series* to celebrate the visual artists of Newfoundland and Labrador, to explore the amazing diversity of their artistic practices, and to give them an opportunity to talk about their work in their own words.

We are an experimental publisher using digital printing technology to discover areas that would not be open to traditional publishers due to cost. We use digital design, on-demand printing and distribution, and social media to reach a worldwide readership at a reasonable price with both print and e-books. We want to use this revolutionary technology to expose a large audience to a wide diversity of art and artists. We plan to examine a broad range of artistic forms: painting, sculpture, fiber art, photography, furniture, jewellery, street art and others; from many different groups of artists. For us at Torbay Bight Press, this will be an exciting journey and we hope it will contribute to a wider appreciation for the grand diversity of art and artists in Newfoundland and Labrador. I am sure there will be some unexpected twists along the way.

Rex Passion
Torbay Bight Press
Torbay, Newfoundland and Labrador
2020

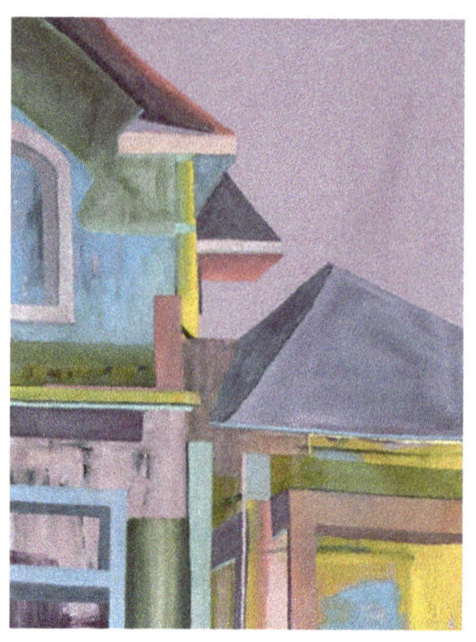

Artist's Statement
2021

My practice explores minimalist architecture using local buildings as subject matter. I select the structures for their unusual angles, intriguing compositions and perspectival planes, as well as their emotional or historical significance. I incorporate house paint, paint chips, and evocative colour names into my work as an examination of the way the material evokes sentiment, memory, and is tied to our concept of home.

Each series builds a sense of place rather than a specific record or detailed portrait, and they act both as a loving reflection and a questioning subversion of this place. My current work is a study of the impact of colour and architecture on the creation of the Newfoundland identity, as well as an exploration of the form and function of Newfoundland houses and their construction of community.

Emily Pittman
St. John's, Newfoundland and Labrador
2021

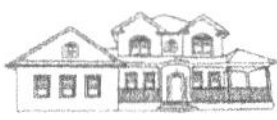

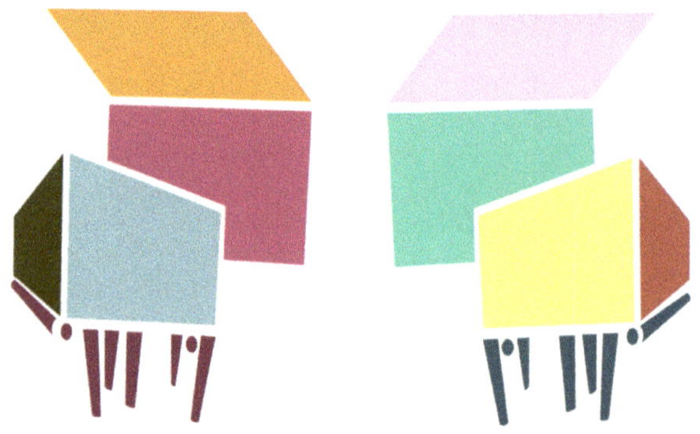

Foreward
by Christina Parker

Emily Pittman captured my attention as an artist the first time I encountered her work. I saw a presentation of her small collages installed in the Newfoundland and Labrador Arts Council Boardroom in 2017. She had just been given the "Adapting Heritage Award" by the Heritage Foundation of Newfoundland and Labrador, and her work was on view there.

I was drawn to Emily's vibrant colour pallet, her minimalist approach to architecture and her use of unorthodox materials. I was convinced that she was an artist I had to work with. Her use of paint chip samples and house paint showed an artist willing to take chances; an artist who had a clear sense of who she was.

Her compositions, a reduction of simple geometry along with bold colour, create works that explore minimalism from a fresh point of view. She isn't interested in representing fully functional buildings, but in creating a 2-D image from a 3-D concept; it is form over function.

Each of Emily's paintings is an exploration of colour and perspective, held together with horizontal and vertical lines that float on a flat surface, bringing harmony and rhythm to the structures she creates. This embodiment of colour is an essential element in how we experience her compositions.

The forms she chooses to work with are architectural fragments selected for their unusual angles and compositions. Initially the buildings appear ordinary but when deconstructed, they reveal unusual and interesting shapes. I am reminded of the work of Piet Mondrian who helped to shape modernism with his method of breaking down and simplifying the architectural plane of his compositions.

When I asked Emily about an artist that she was inspired by as a student, she named Josef Albers, who taught at the Bauhaus. Albers was a master theorist of how we see and experience colour and I am reminded of his aesthetics in Emily's work, with her use of lines and blocks of vivid colour to reveal shape and form.

Much more than solid structure, her paintings also have a dream-like quality, an inventive re-imagining of the idea of home, that invites us to picture ideal places and how we identify with them. Possibilities emerge where structures that don't naturally fit together, exist in harmony through line and colour. The dream home becomes a state of mind where anything is possible. Pittman takes the traditional idea of home and turns it on its ear.

Someday Homes Fill My Dreams follows the trajectory of Emily Pittman's art practice from 2017 to the present. We see how she has expanded her sense of place and identity to produce the finest work of her career. This publication allows a rare opportunity to follow an artist from her first post-art-school public exhibition, to her development into an important artist who chooses to live and work in Newfoundland and Labrador.

Someday Homes

Fill My Dreams

If you want to see the blue sky above

while you're sipping tea

or feel your hair wave in a summer breeze

while staying safe on the other side of the door

this is the one you've been waiting for

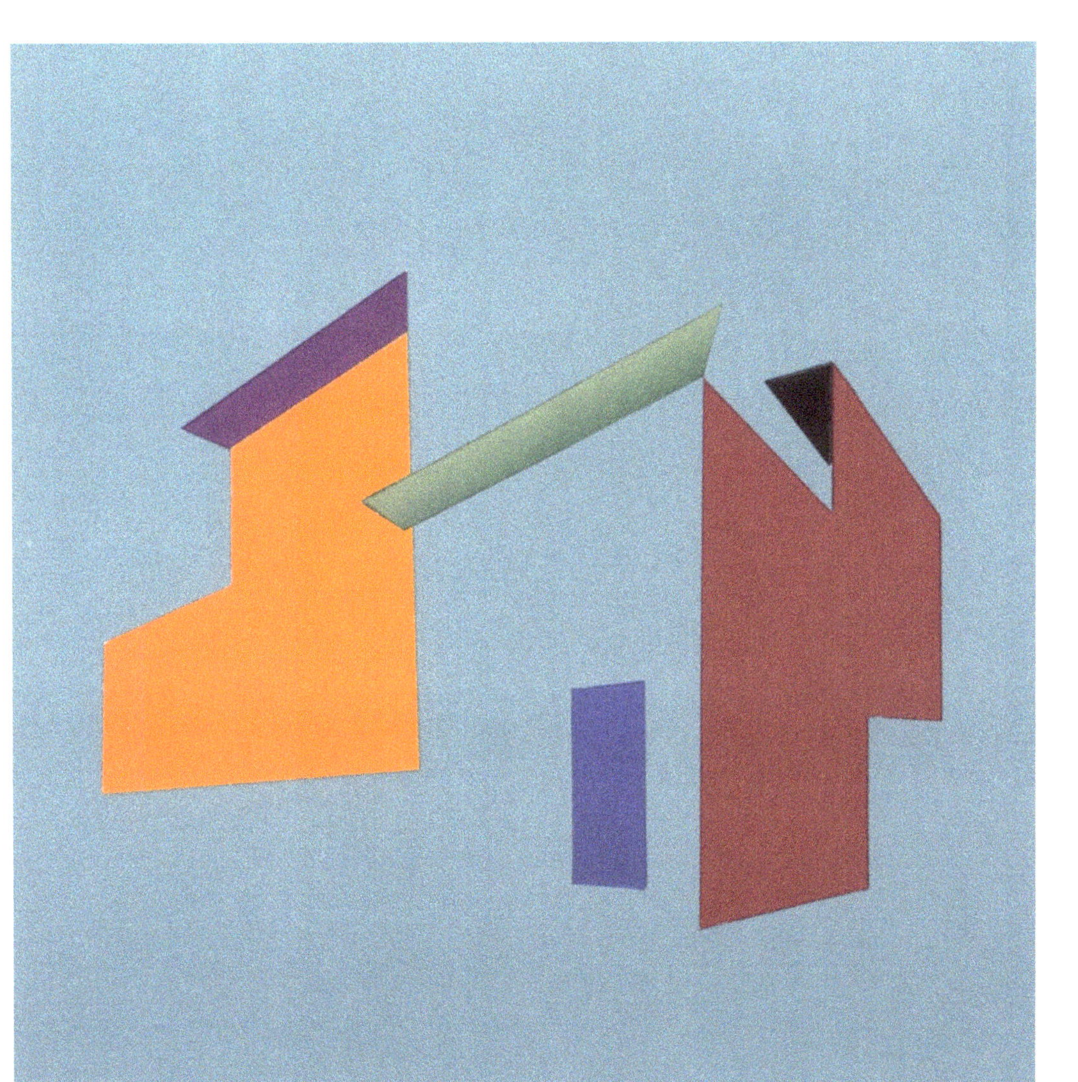

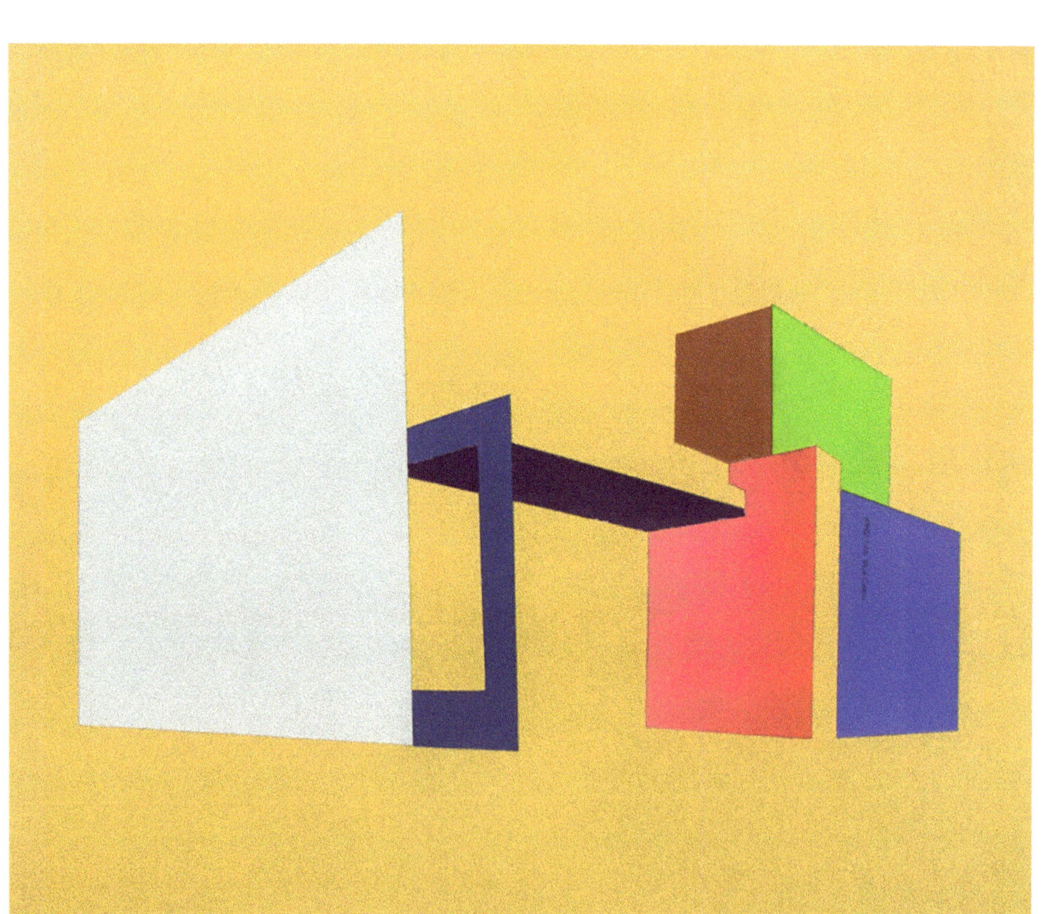

A slice of purple connecting me and you

holding on for dear life with a bit of blue

Crisp and clean, lighter than air,

we're invited inside the sheltered step

with a royal red floor.

A pastel recipe for beautiful dreams,

this dainty dwelling sings a sweet song of hope.

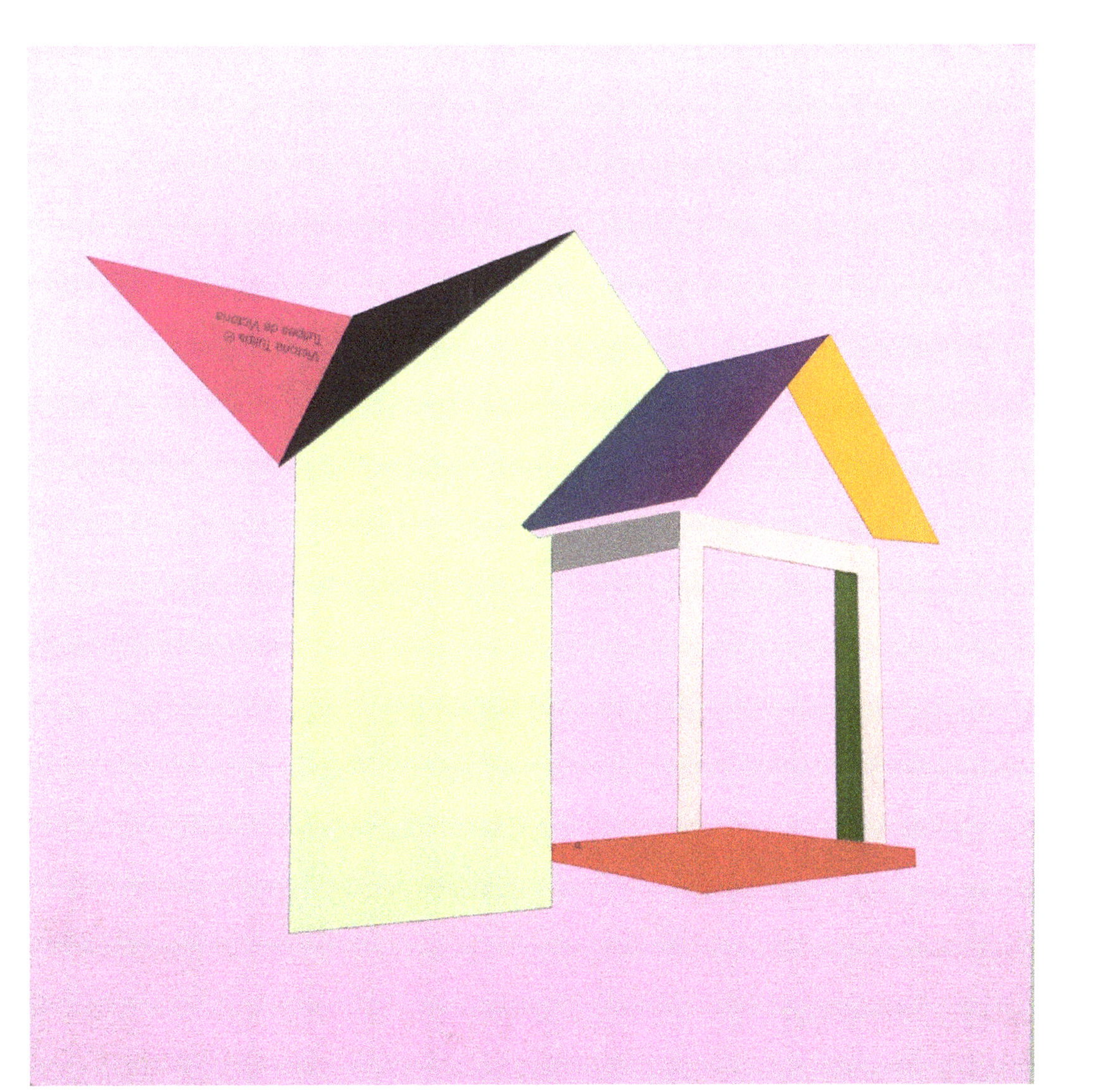

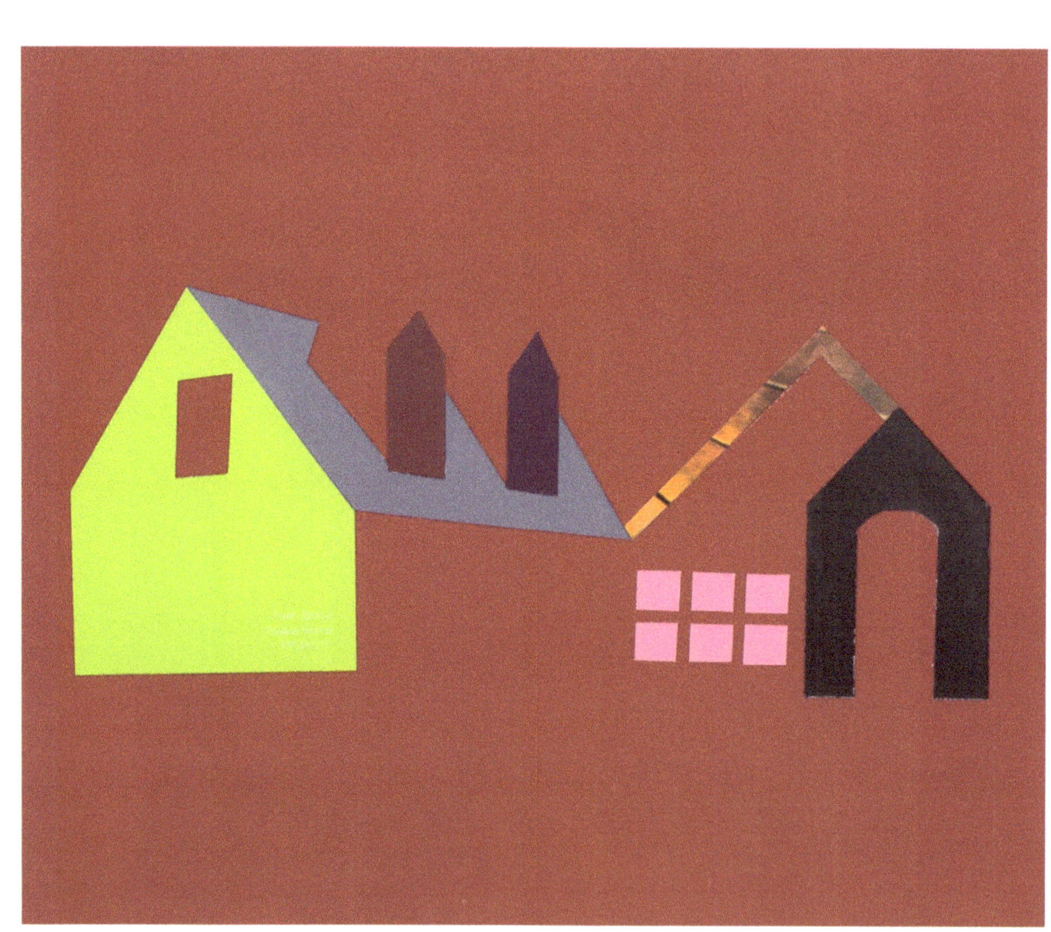

It looks perfect now, but just *you* wait.
The sink *will* be filled *with* Red Rose stains
and the ornate tiles *will* be caked *with* mud
from the garden *you* couldn't get enough of.

Out and in, out and in,

shrinking backwards

then coming forward into my space again.

My room is hanging on by a fiery pink thread,

and the door is open and gaping,

 imploring you to drive through.

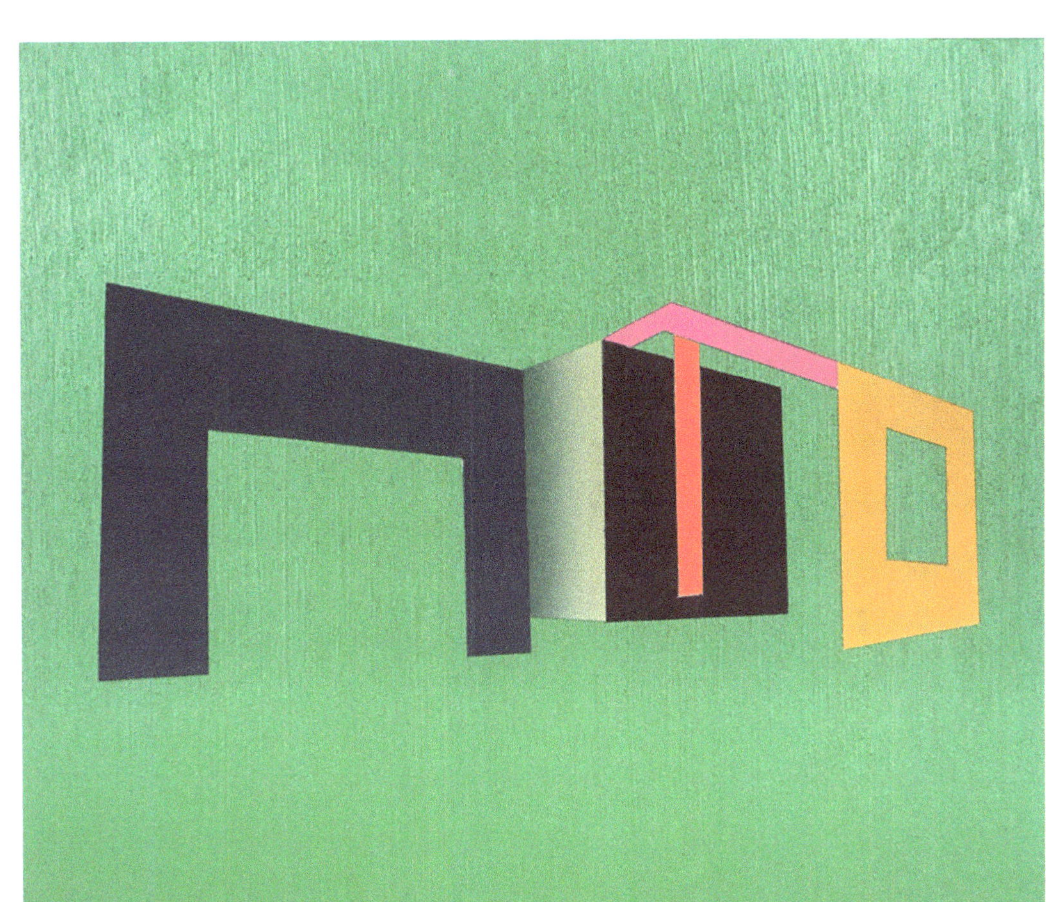

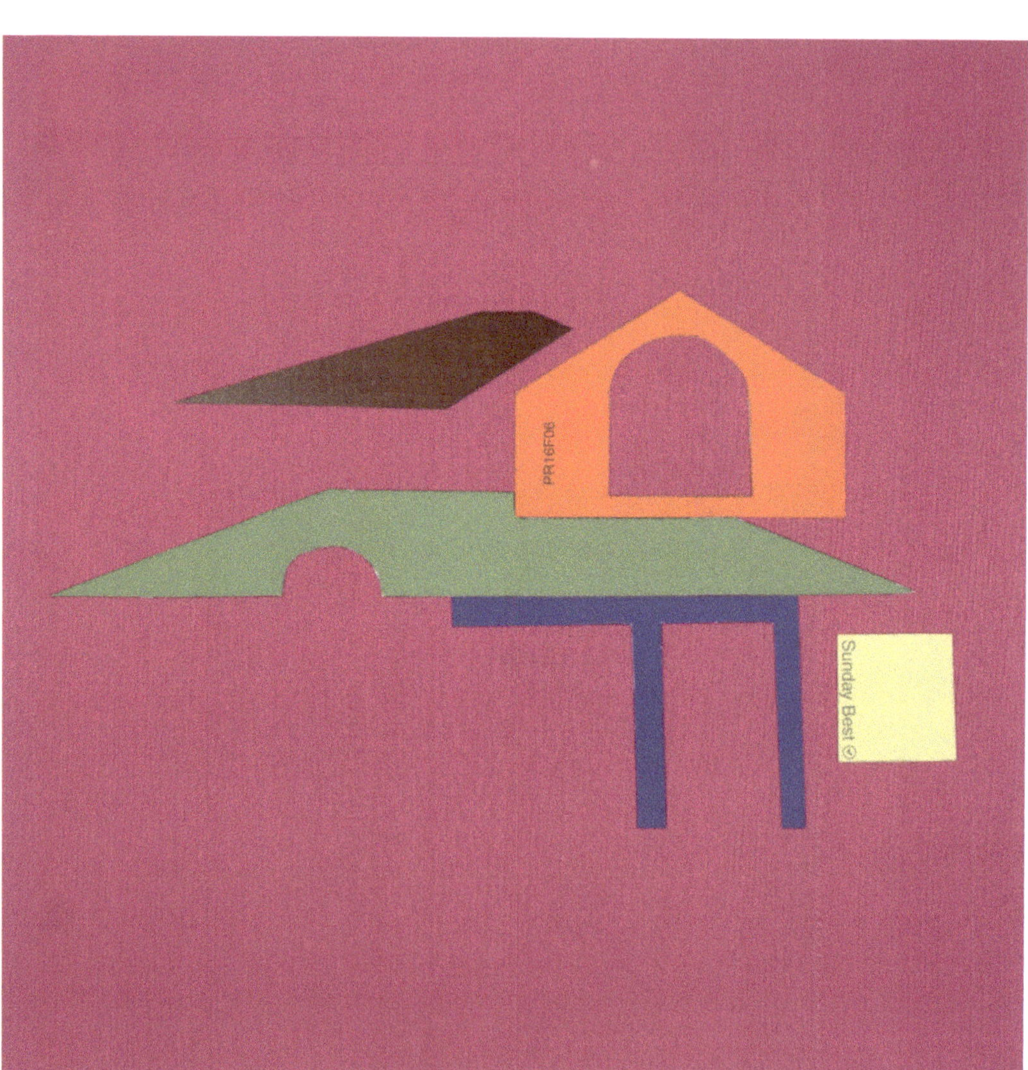
PR16F06
Sunday Best ©

With rose-coloured faith,

I stand on my own two feet.

A close up view of a place you knew;

we don't visit home for the house.

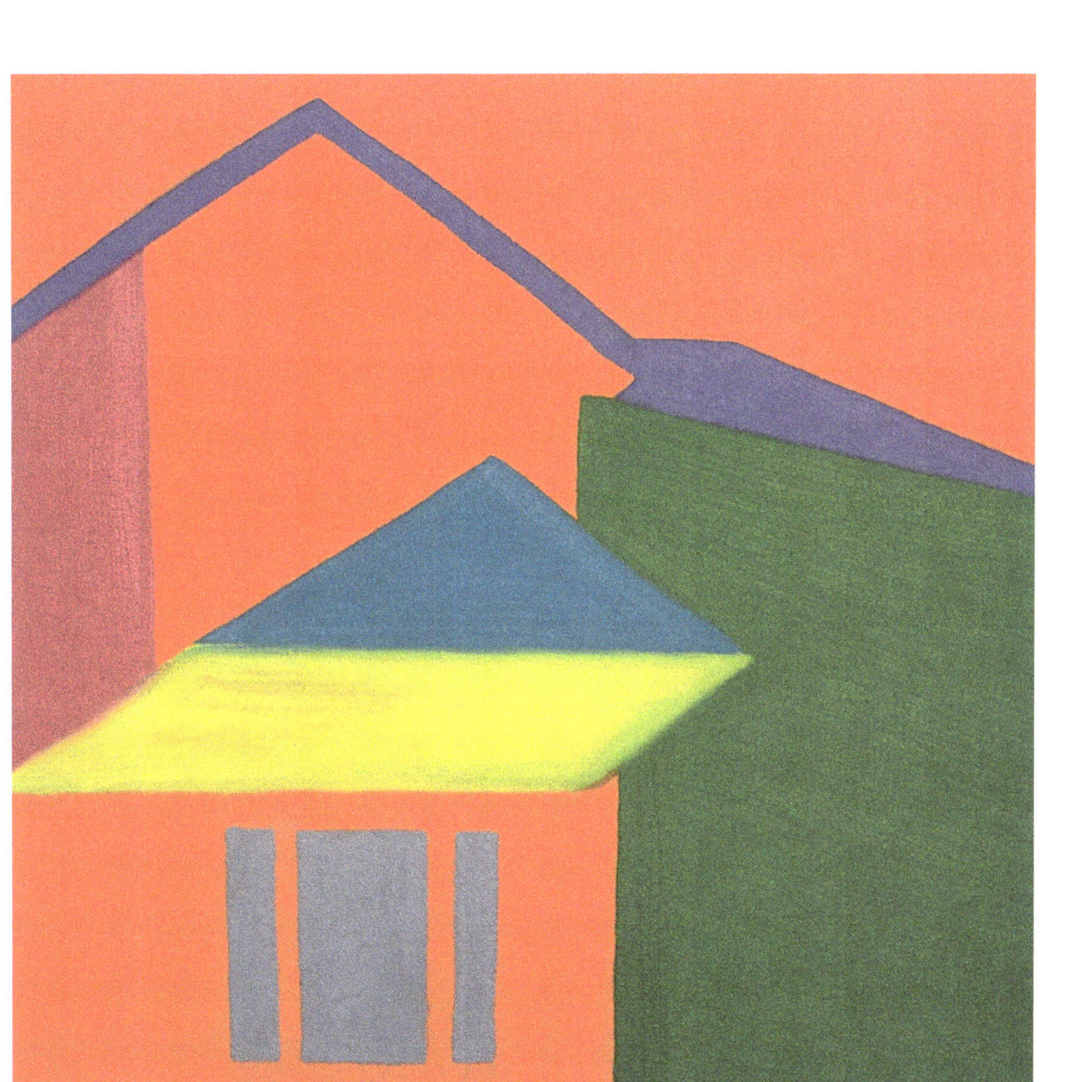

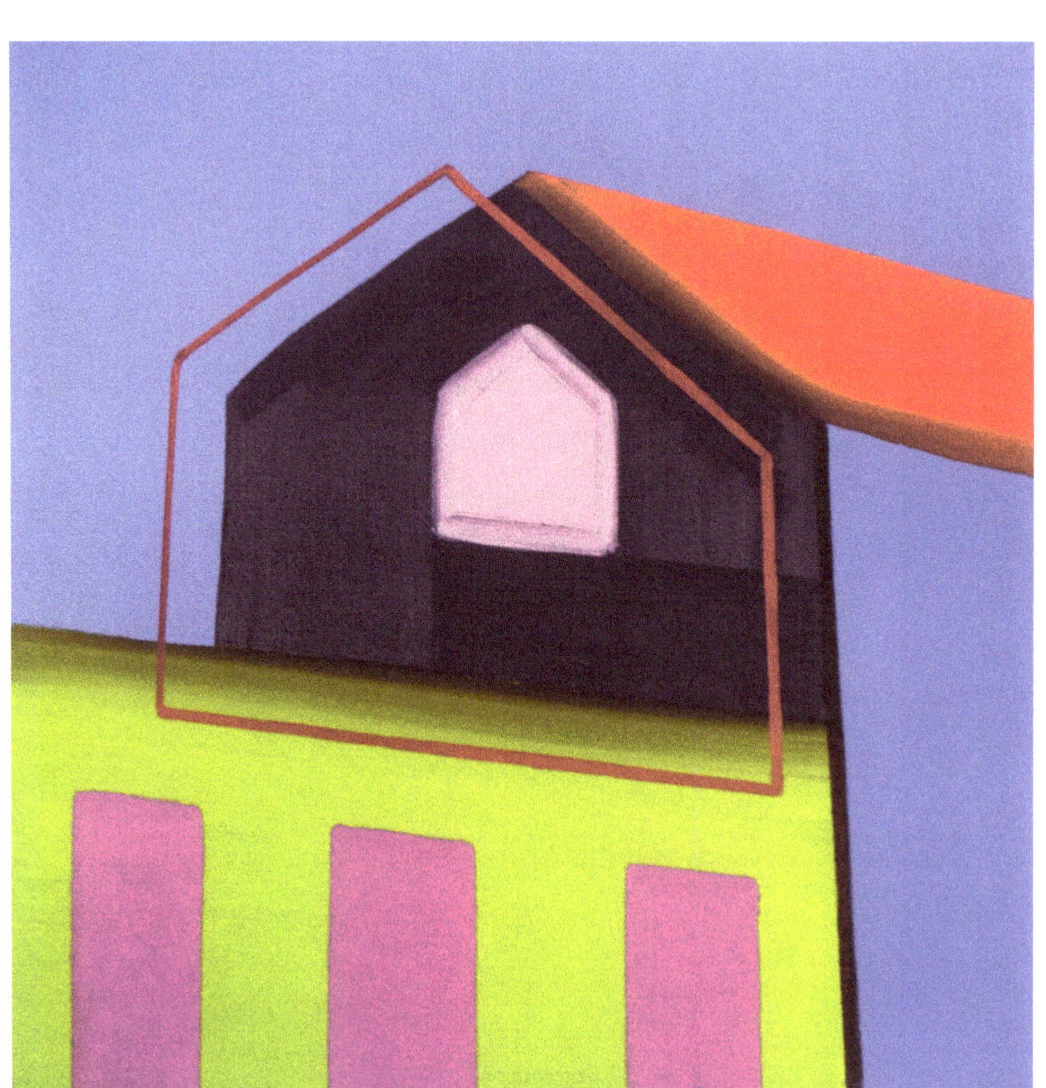

A red thread with no loose end,

or a trail leading me out,

not unchanged,

then back from *where* I came.

Magenta playfulls curl across glowing yellow
and are halted by a line,
thin but heavy.

The weight of the roof teeters on a precipice,
steadied by a contour.

A circle looks out from the shelter,
giving way to a cool blue
softly signalling the end of one space
and the start of another.

An empty window waits to be filled with smiling faces,
waving at walkers-by.

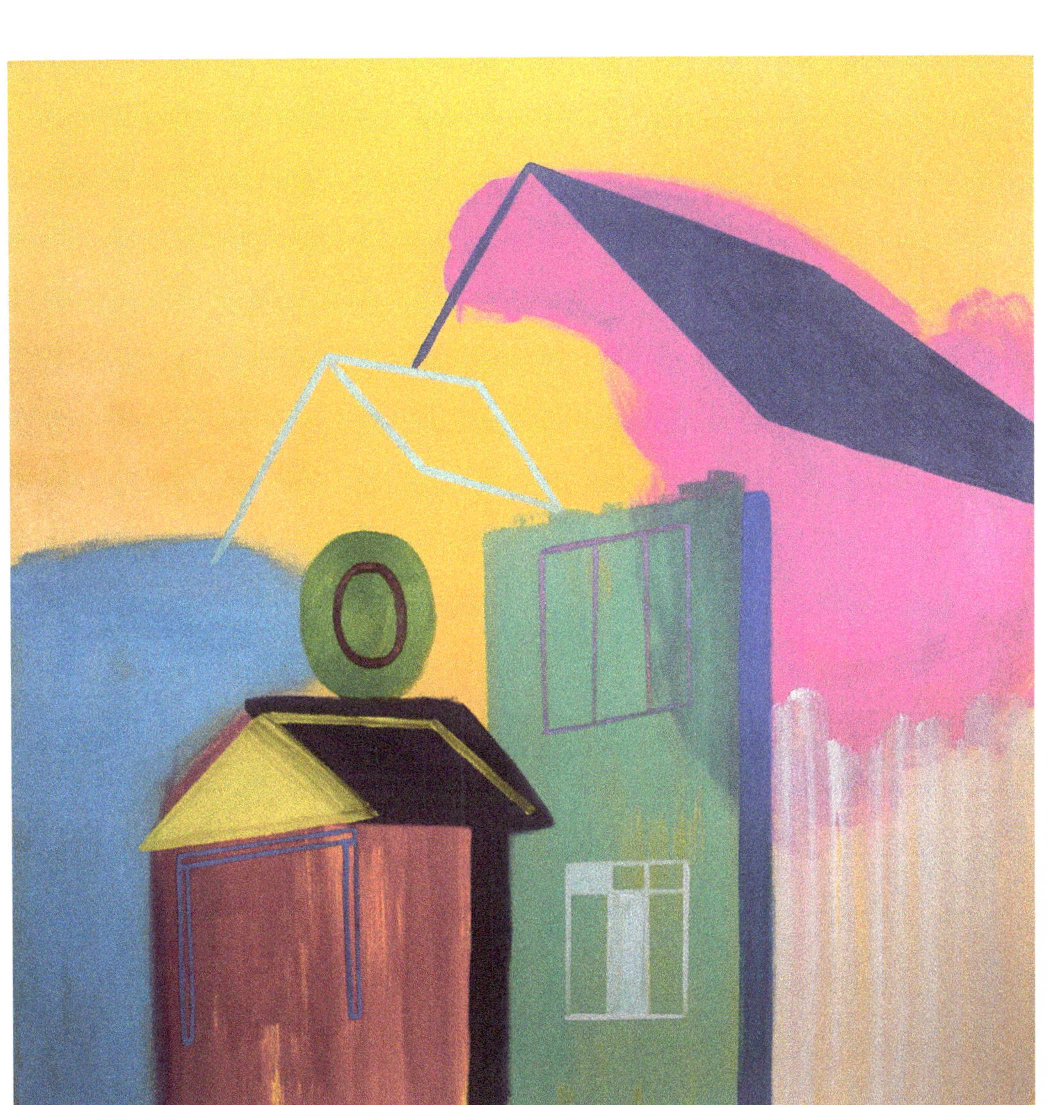

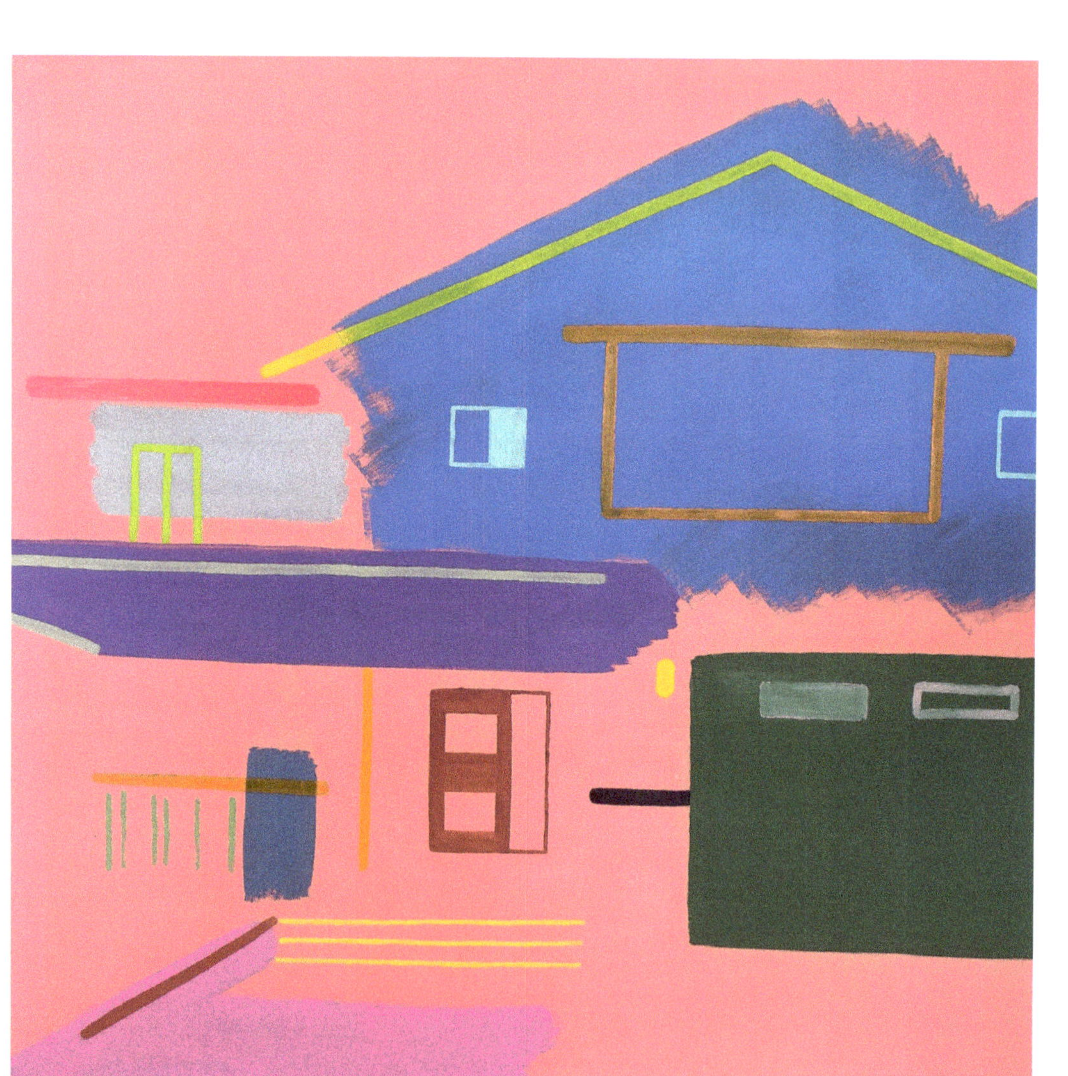

The door hangs in sticky bubblegum pink.

A yellow light blinks

and stays out of the fight between blue and green,

one a restful place to rise above the day

and the other ready to open wide

for a speedy getaway.

Escape on foot is a lost cause,

the stairs are surely out of the question,

and there's nothing to grasp

when the world becomes slick with ice,

with the lilac just begging to sweep you off the surface.

My mom's shade of blue

Building fragments piece by piece

Into something new.

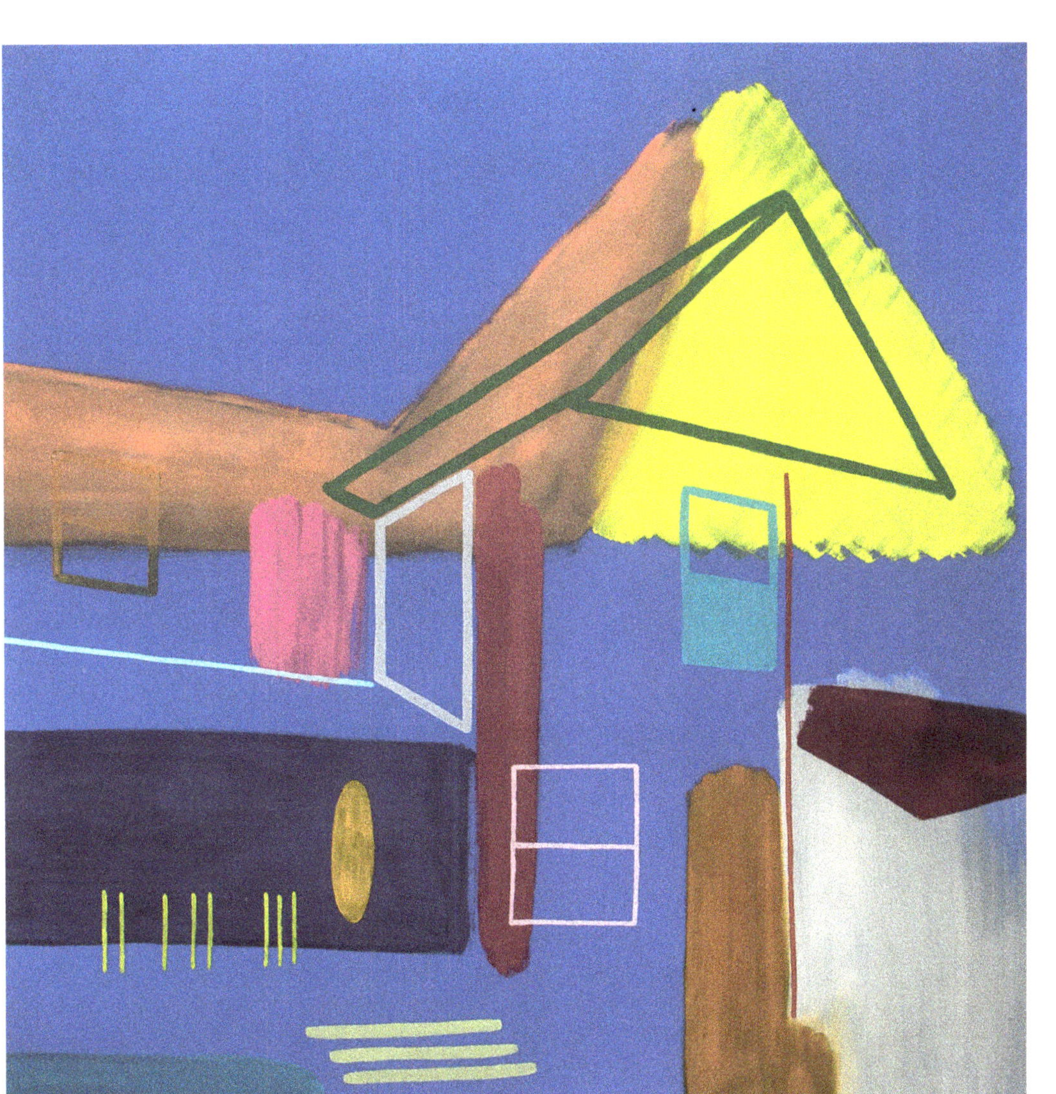

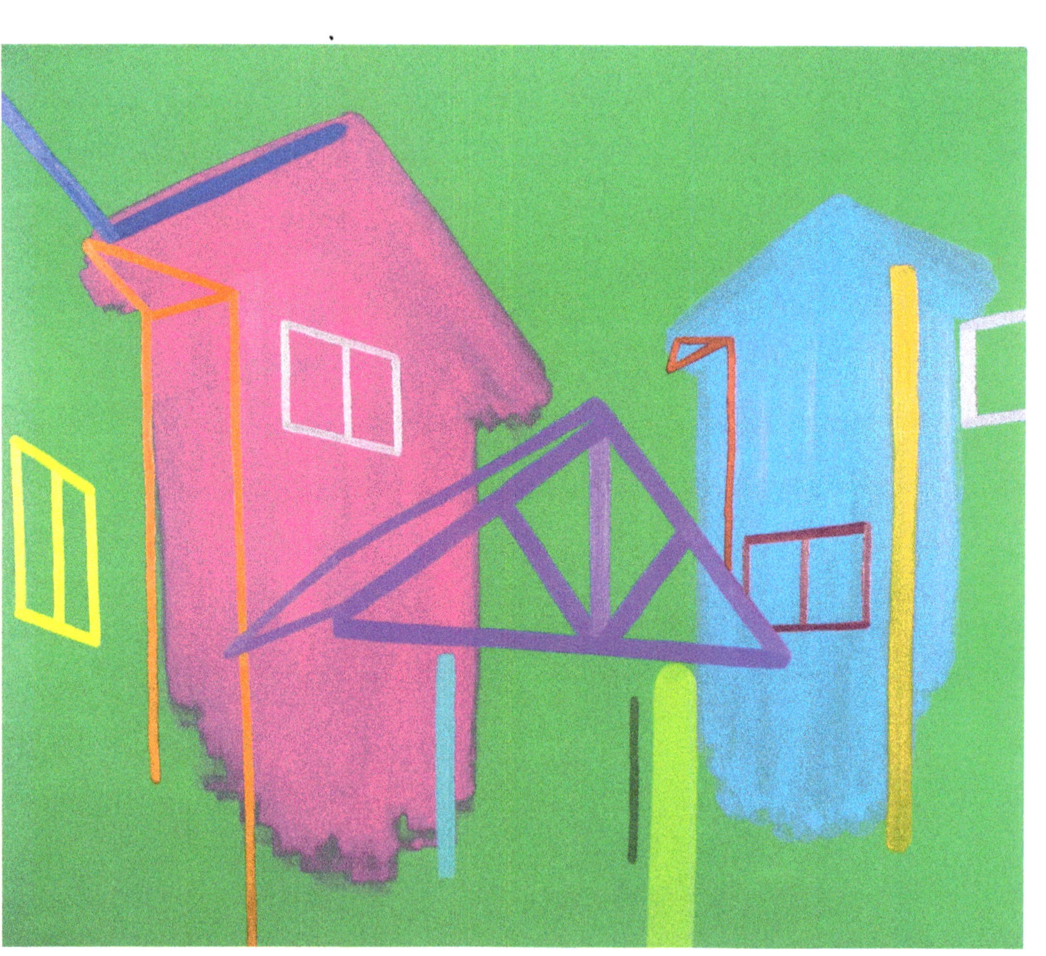

A memory just be*y*ond m*y* fingertips,

shifting into place line b*y* line.

A photograph *w*ith curling corners

hanging in m*y* mind.

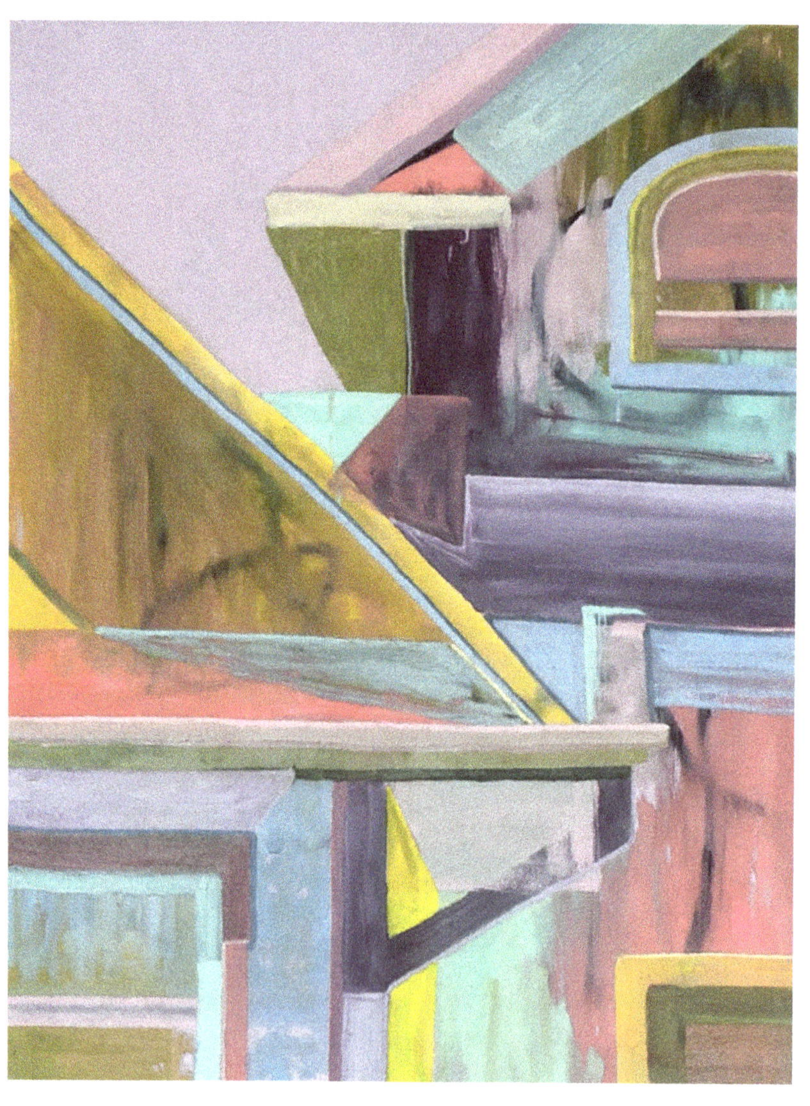

This house is only purple

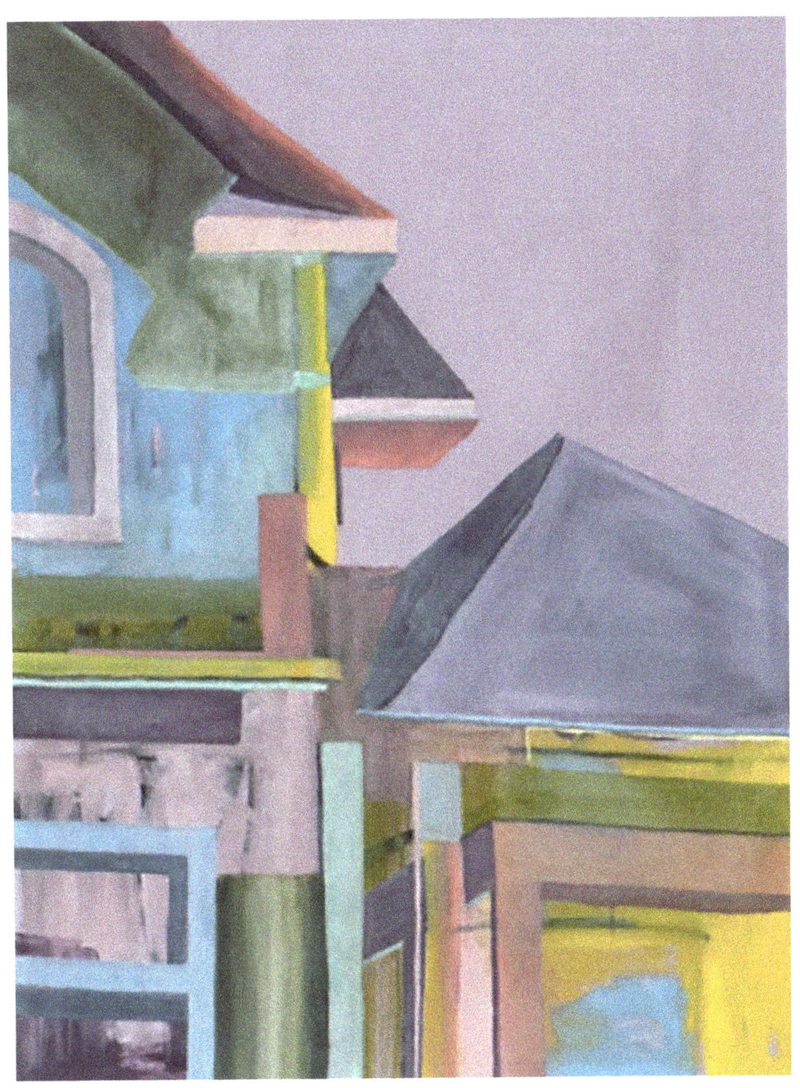

in my head

Neighbours

one balancing on a precarious stage

and another stocky and square,

in floating stability,

play well together in Little Heart's Ease.

A fresh coat of paint is all that was needed

to bring these two together again,

shy at first but now inseparable.

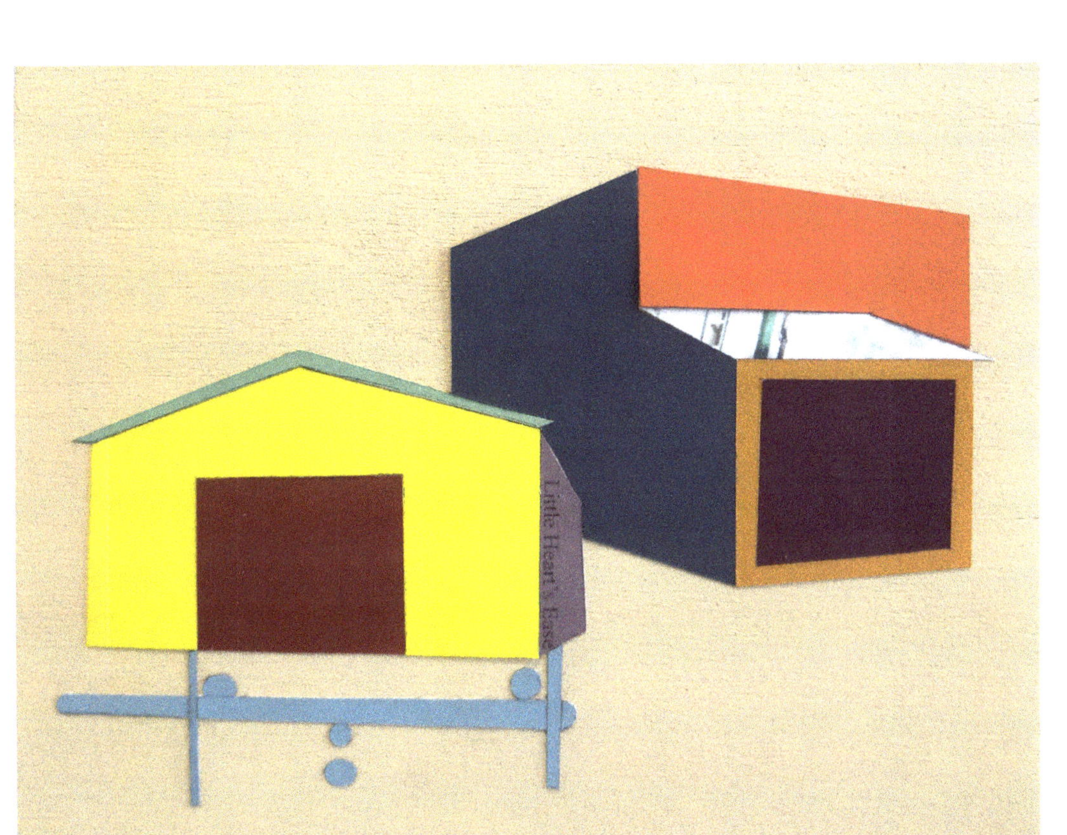
Little Heart's Ease

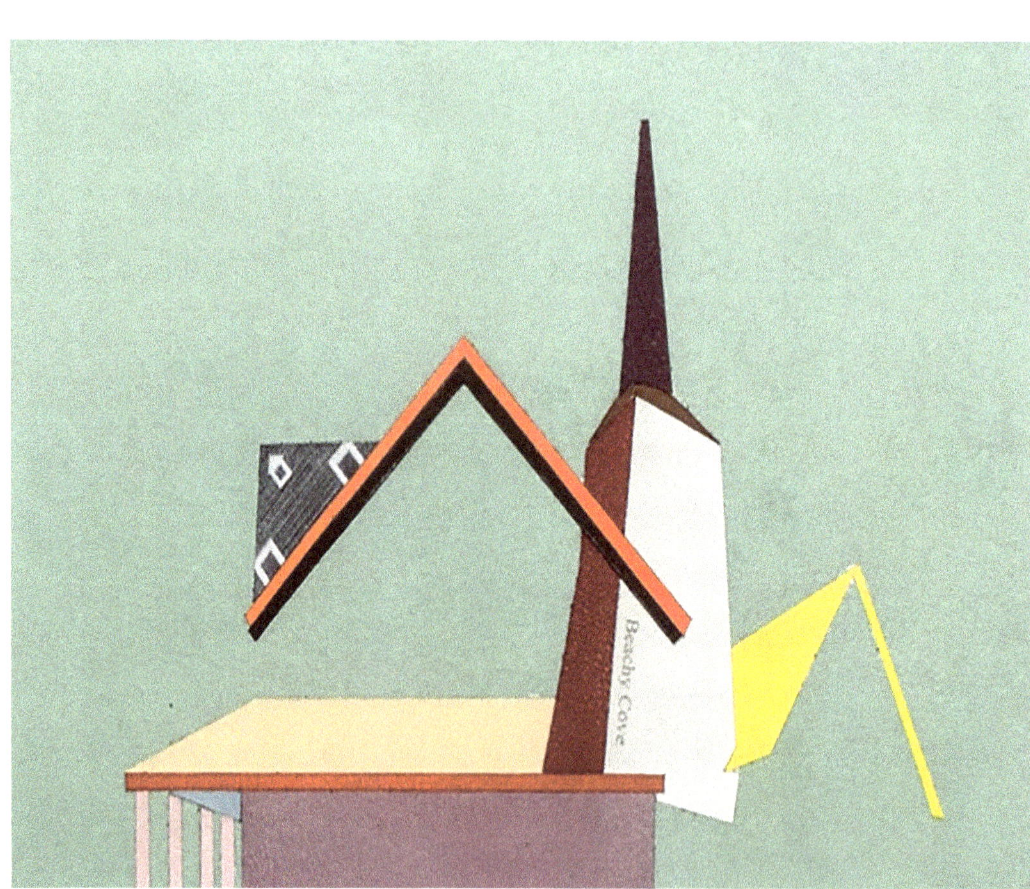
Beachy Cove

A holy home

held together by sheer willpower

Neighbors

unacquainted yet intertwined

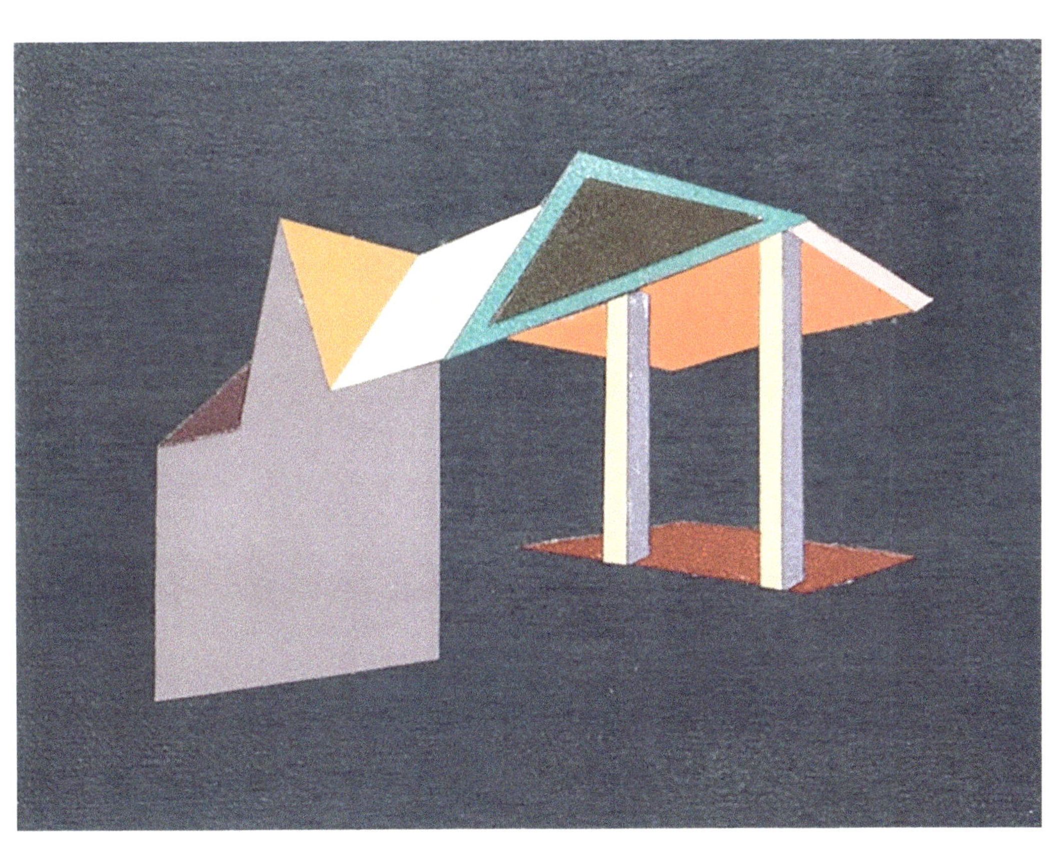

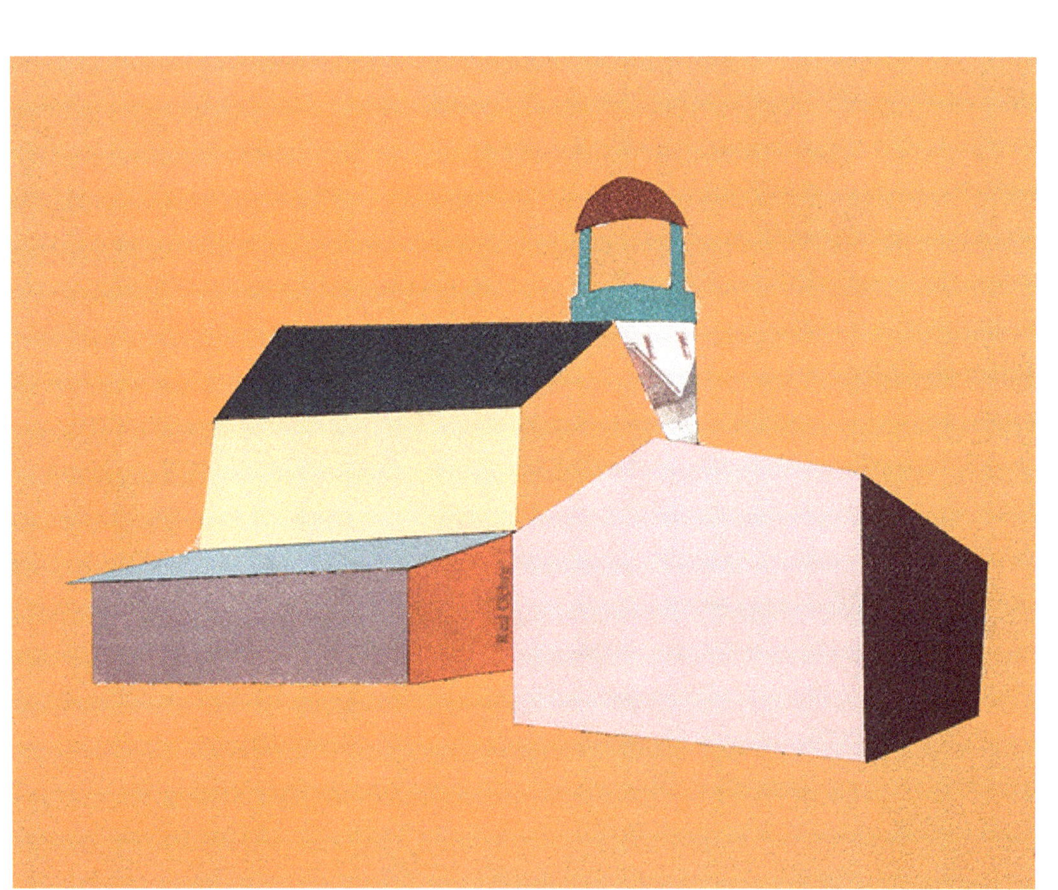
Red Ochre

A landlocked lookout calls me its keeper,

securing *my* safe arrival in the *navy* night.

I travel far and then turn for home

into a beam of golden light.

Standing side by side

Supported from above and

Held up from below

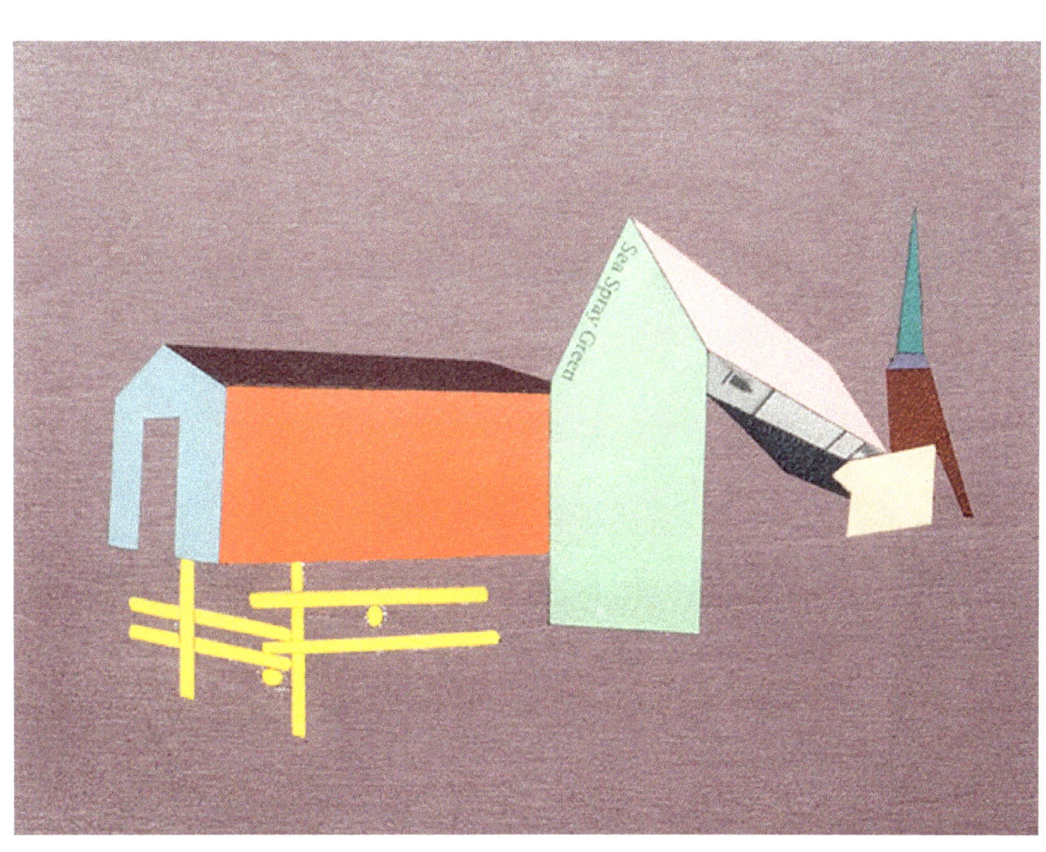
Sea Spray Green

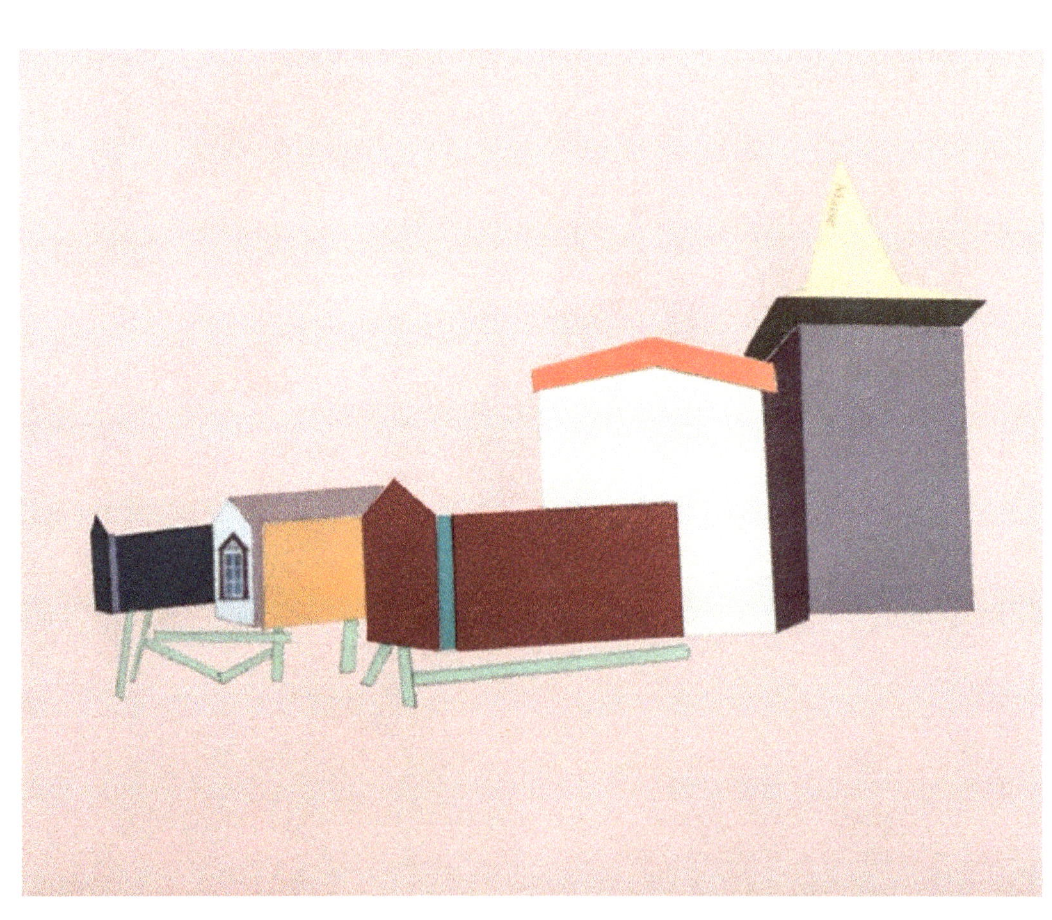

Legs dripping in sea foam green,

they drift together and knock knees.

Collisions between their carefully cut edges are

persuaded by each gentle push,

until they are drumming

sporadic thuds for the dancing water.

A balancing act, above and below,

joined together with periwinkle blue.

The a-line crow's nest waits for red alert,

trusting his brother and his base

to keep him from a short slide

and a clean break.

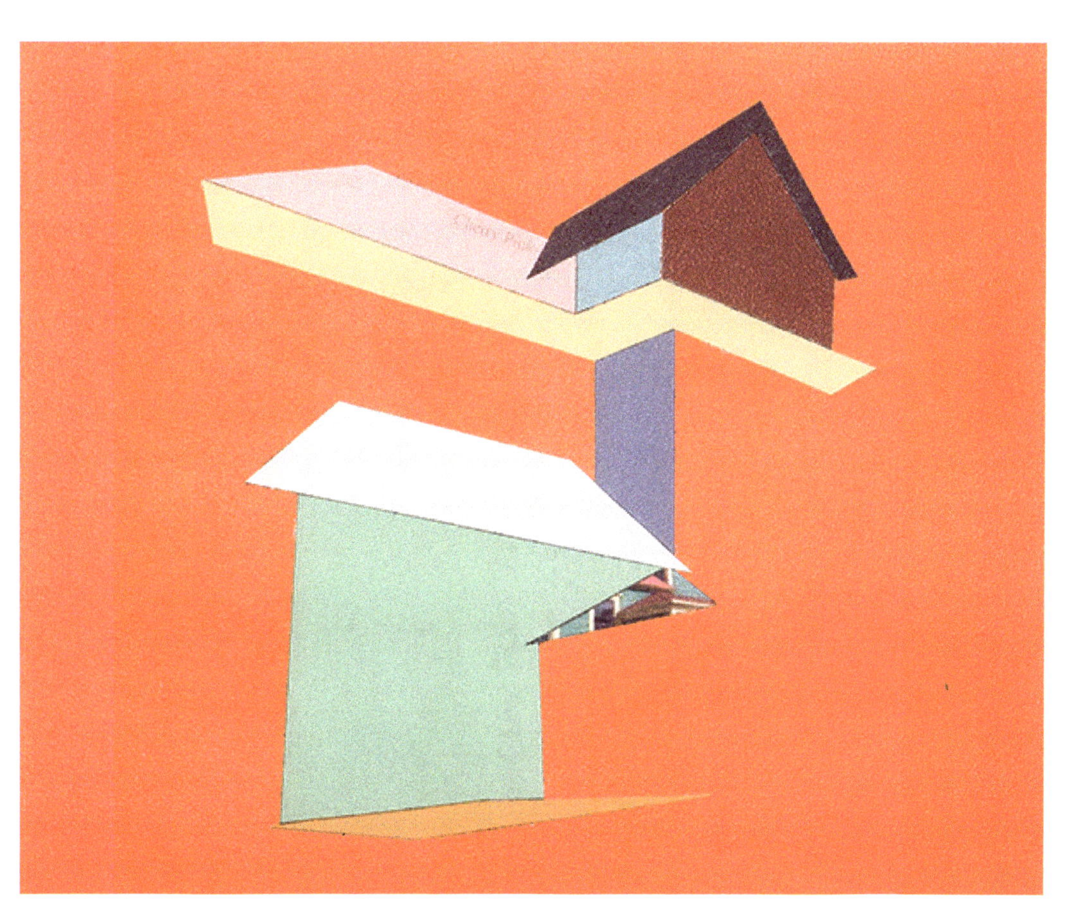

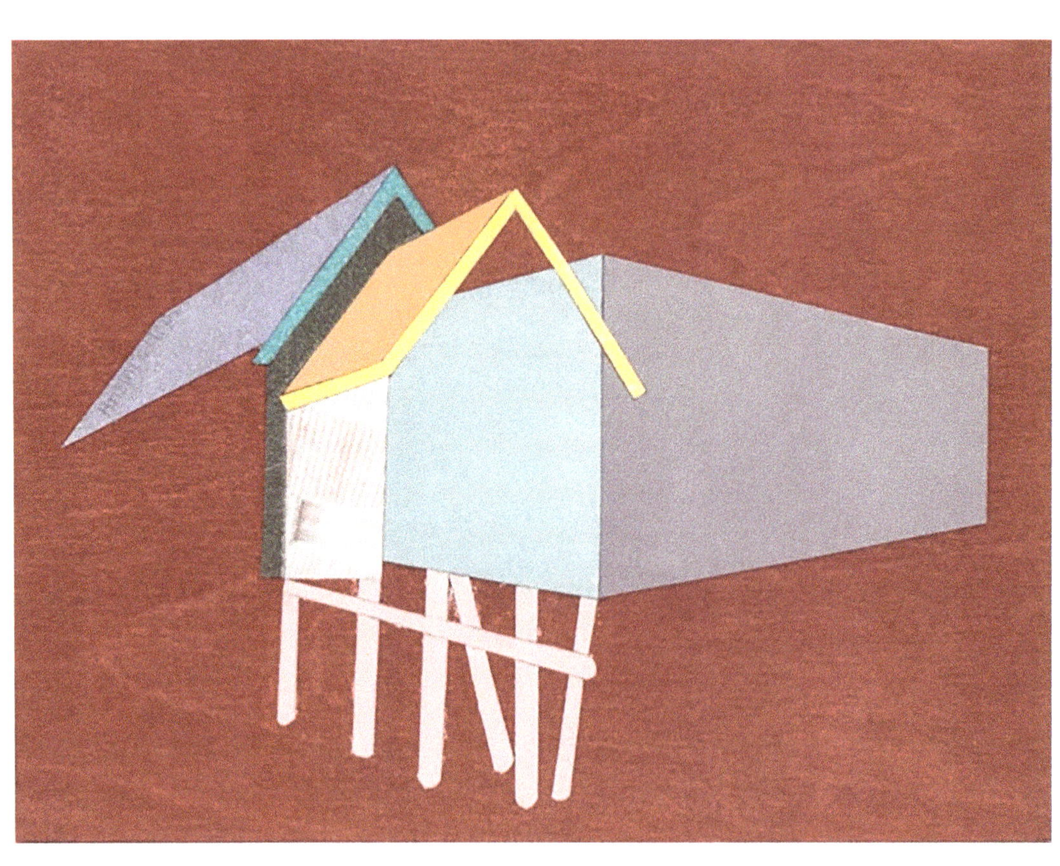

On its last legs

*w*aiting for the other shoe to drop

A yellow glow pushes its *way* through

to save the dreary day,

unaffected by the proud royal blue

or the charming red line.

The gold seeps through them all and binds us.

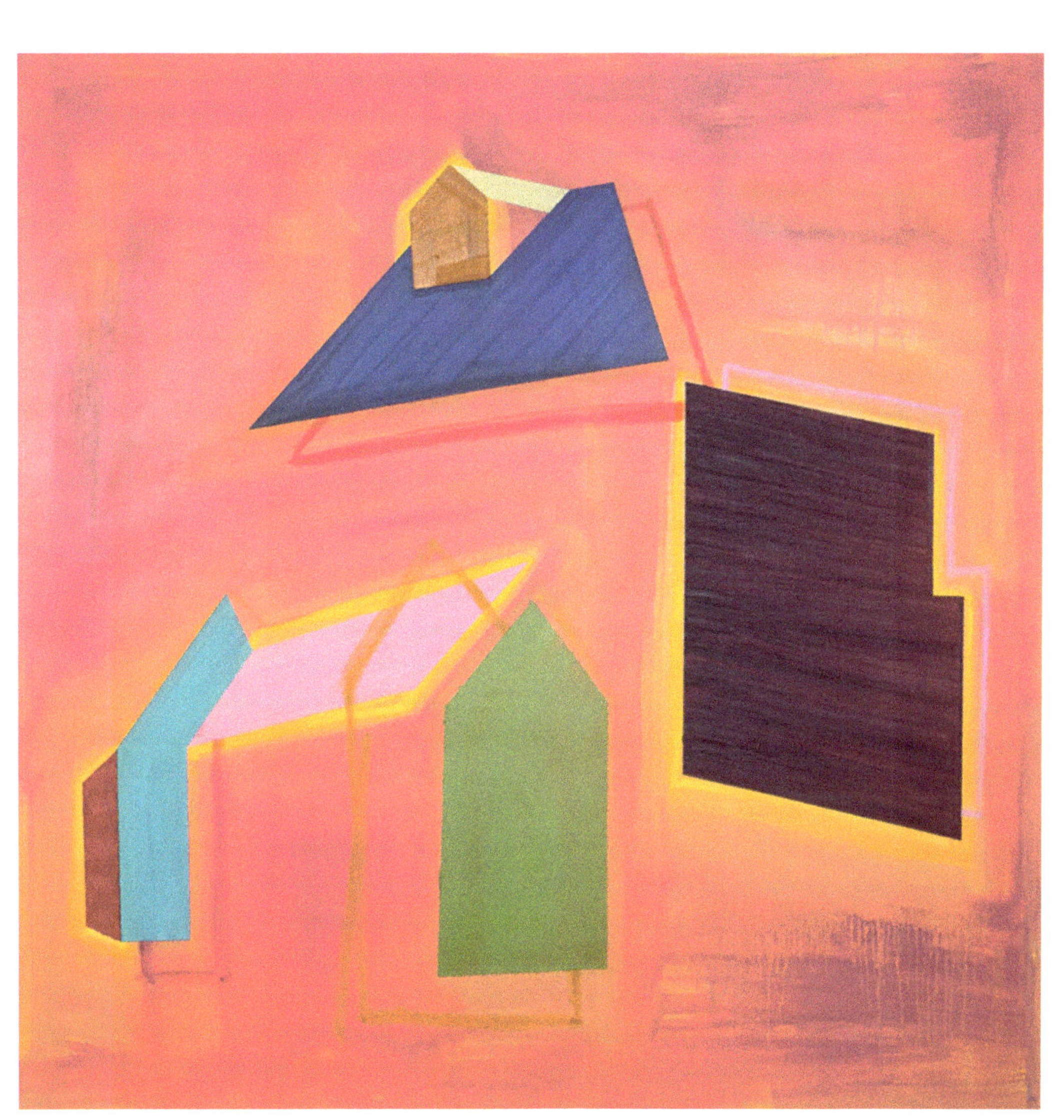

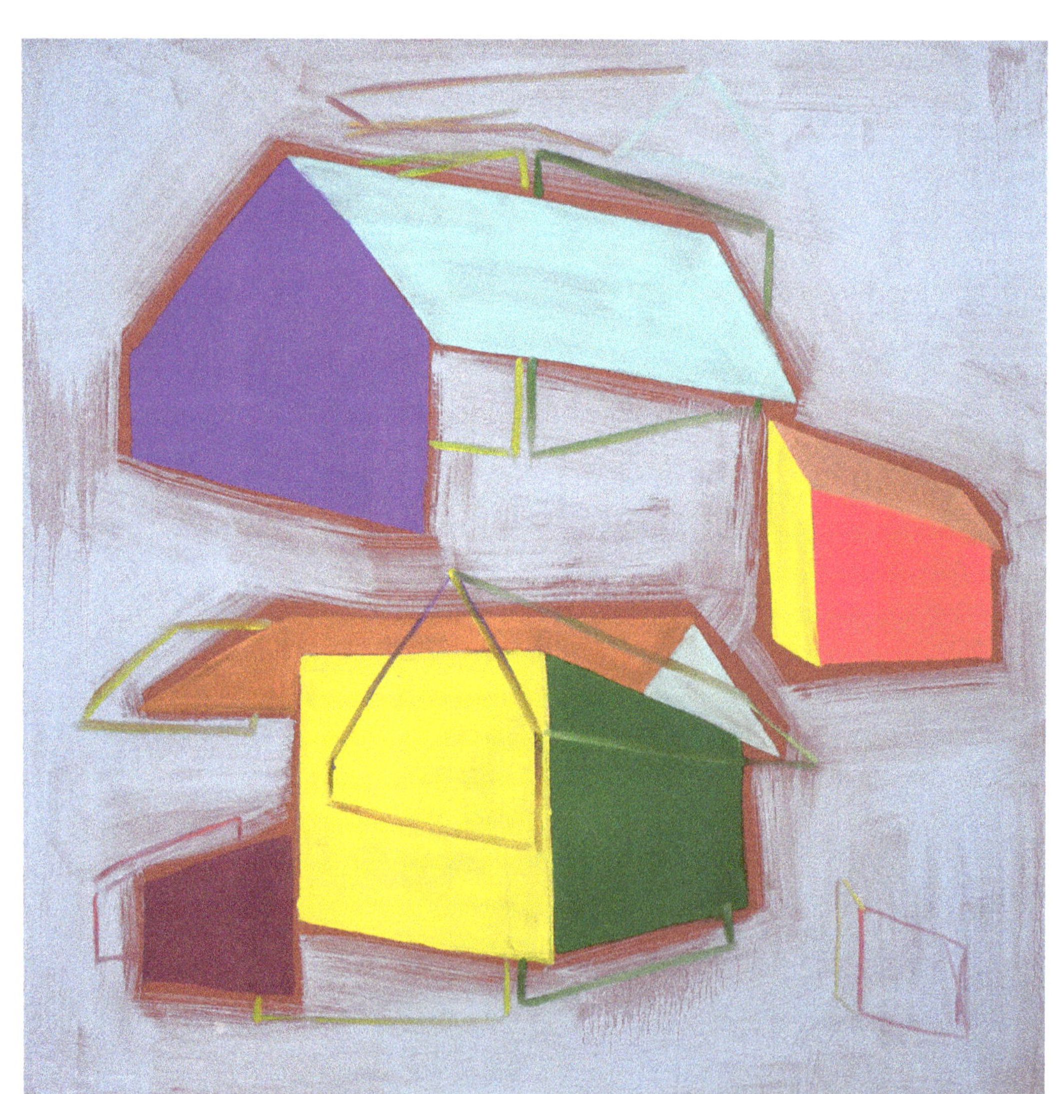

I leave a mark at *every* place I've been

or does it leave a mark on me?

The past seeps through the cracks

of these crooked walls,

what was frozen now thaws

and facing the truth of my foundational flaws

is easier done alone than said aloud.

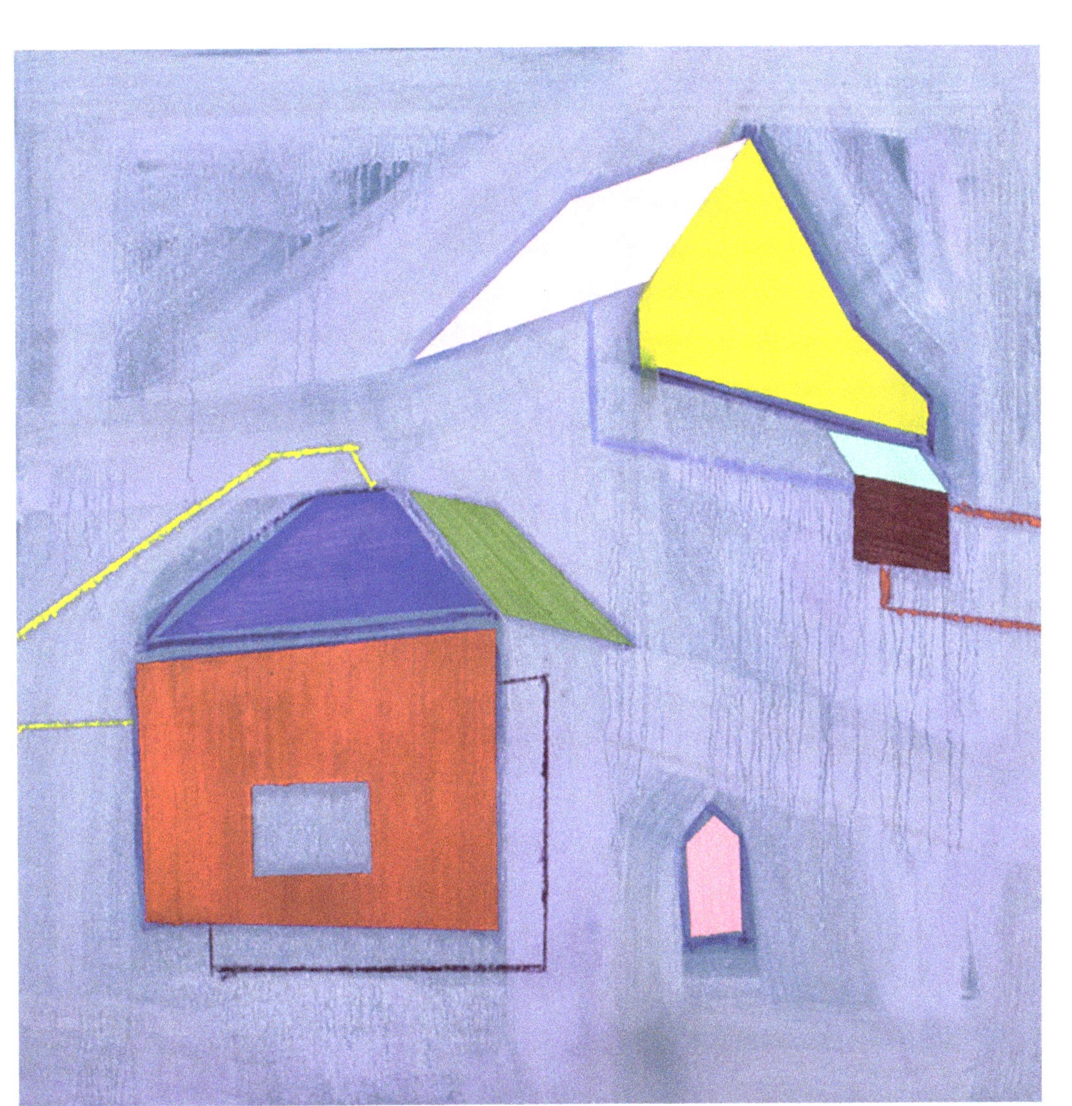

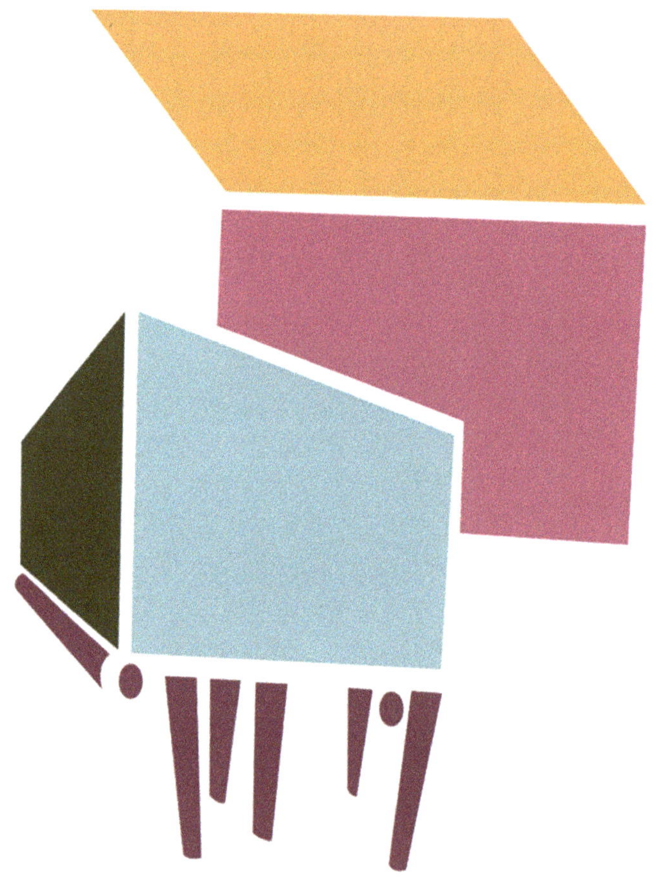

Legs dangling in the water

the *waves wrap* around *my* feet

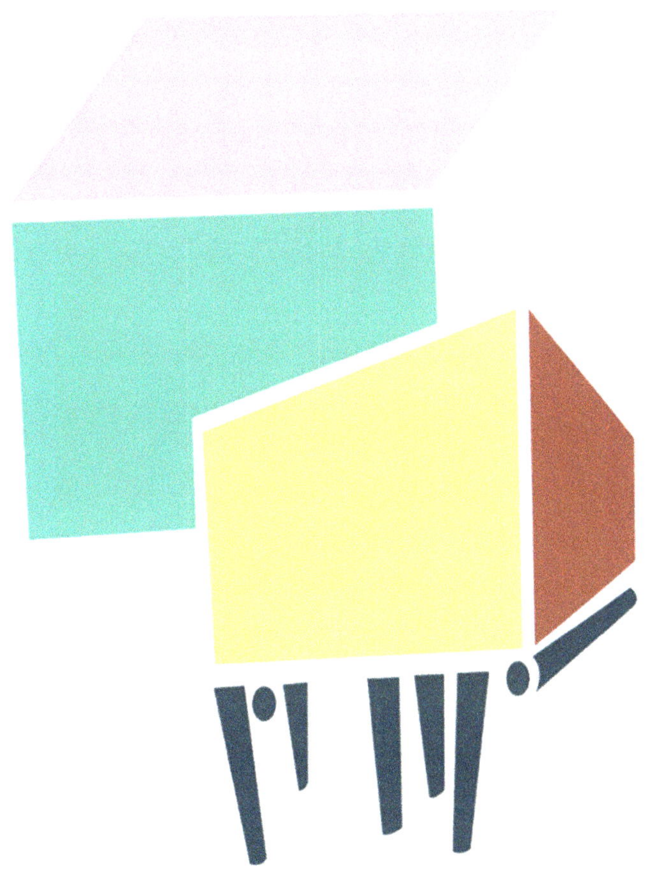

on a hot summer day,

and beg to pull me away.

A pink sky hovers

I add one box more

until It threatens to fall

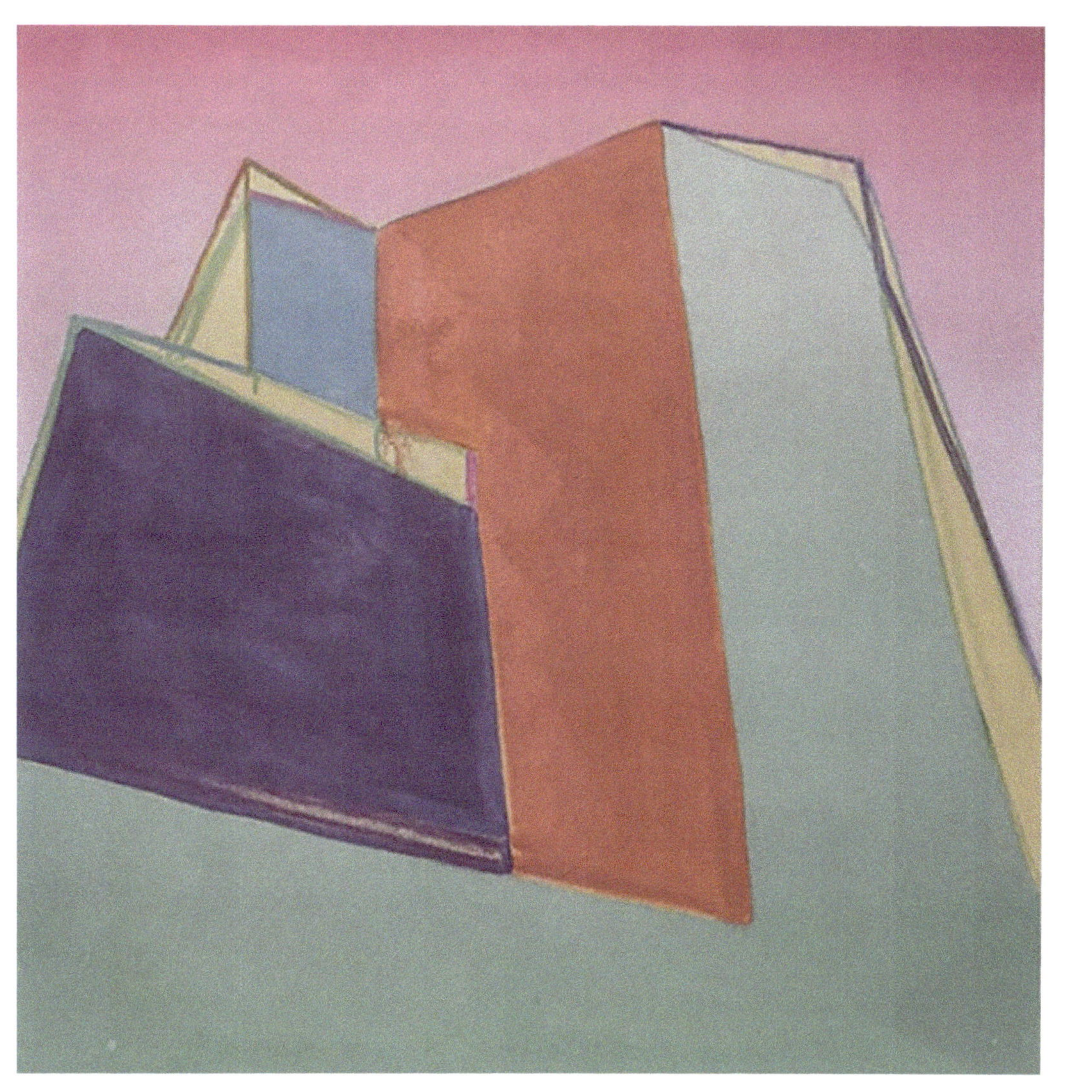

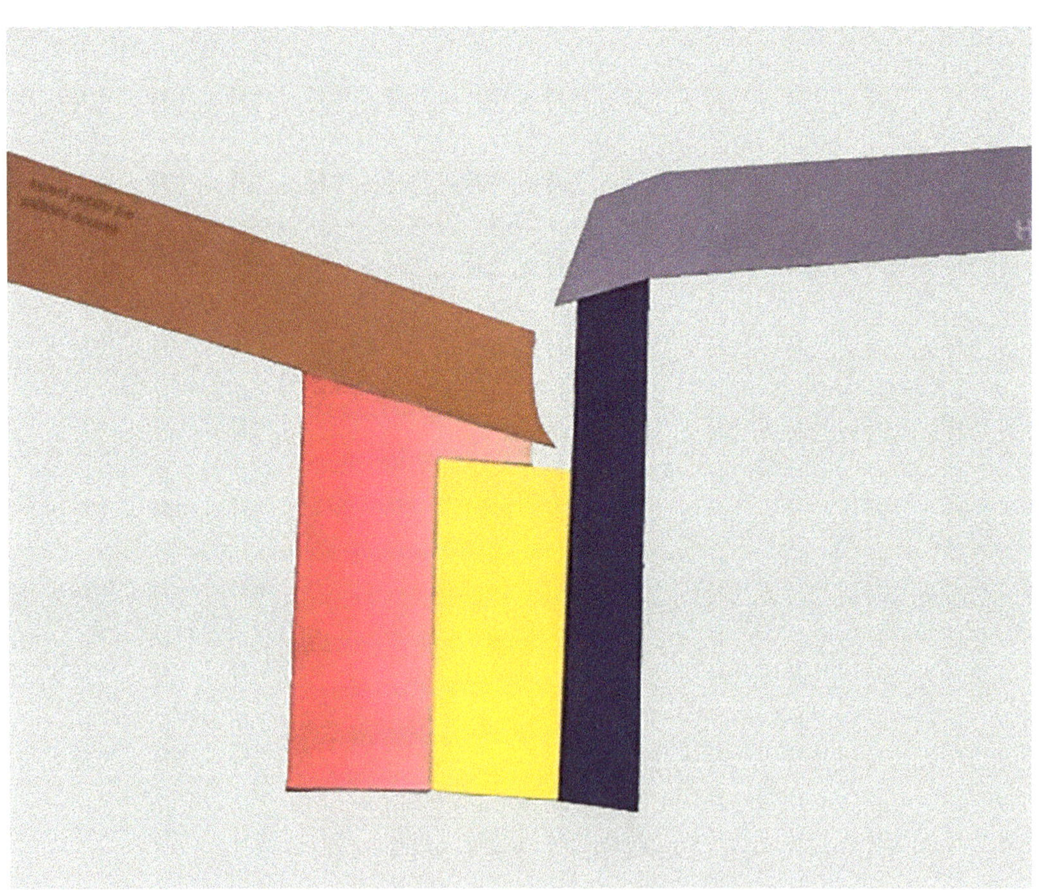

Straining to keep the rain away

from our own little slice of sunshine

Tall and proud

I am invited inside

through the pear green door

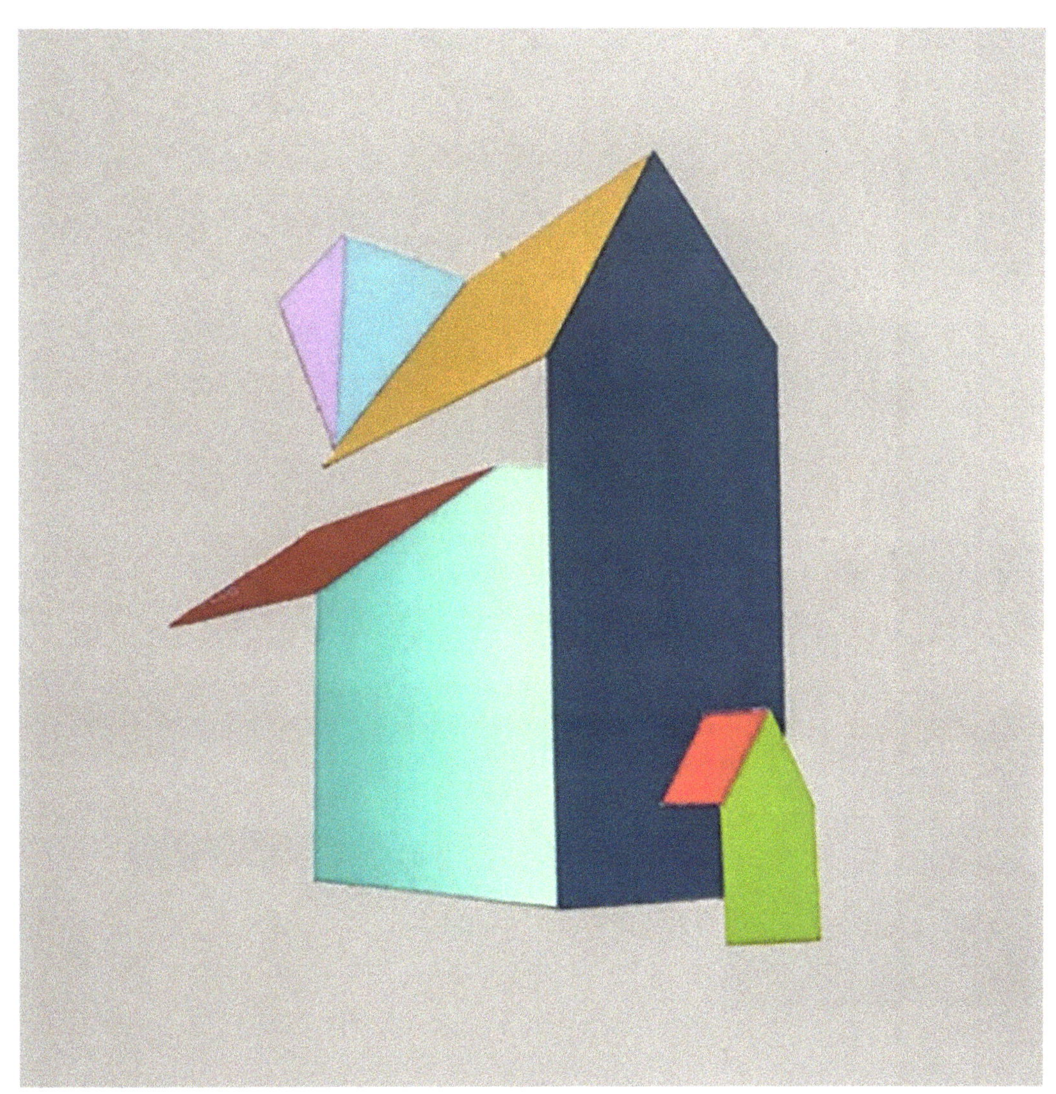

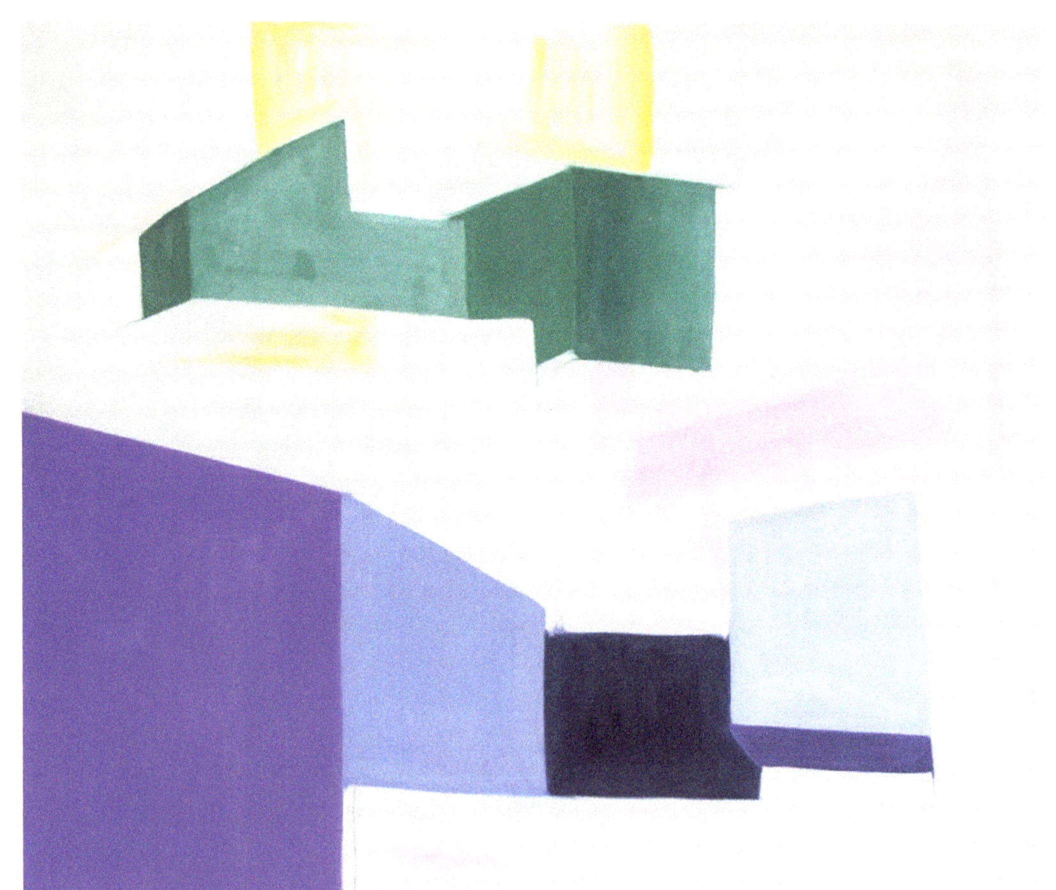

I can't keep every house I've ever loved

while still having room to live

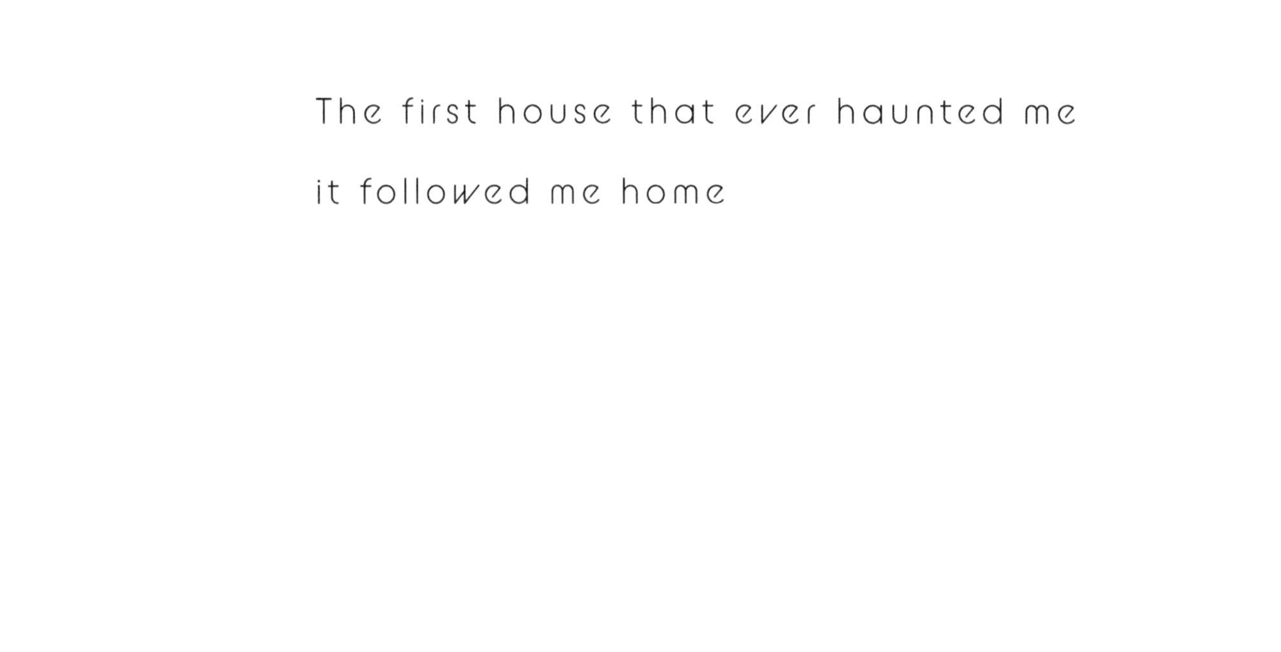
The first house that ever haunted me

it followed me home

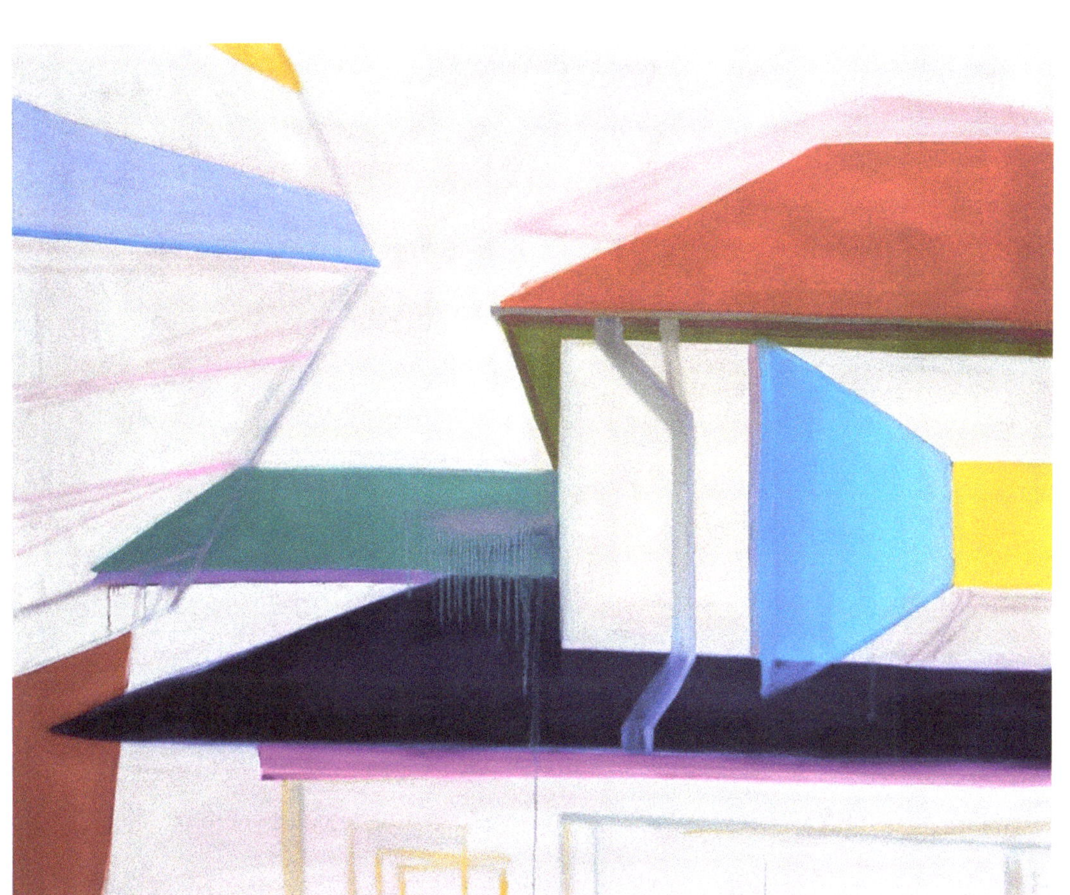

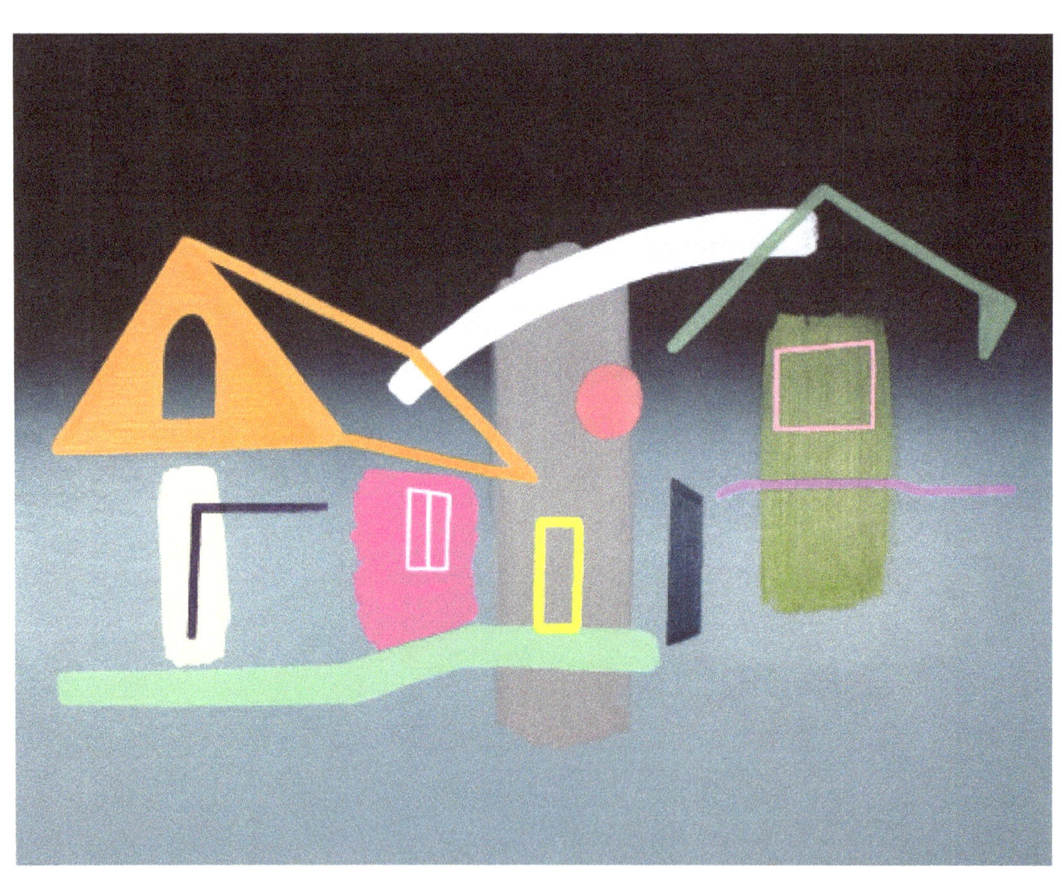

Darkness falls on the *water*,

rolling black as far as *we* can see.

The edges of our *windows* glow

through the curtains hung to keep out the cold.

A garden lit path leads the *way* back home,

drinking up the drips from our moonlit dip

and music pours from the open door,

inviting us to keep *away* sleep just a little longer.

Full to the brim with memories,

a seedling we planted now a towering tree.

Creating space as we grew,

one patch of red and another of blue,

building our lives around a lopsided view.

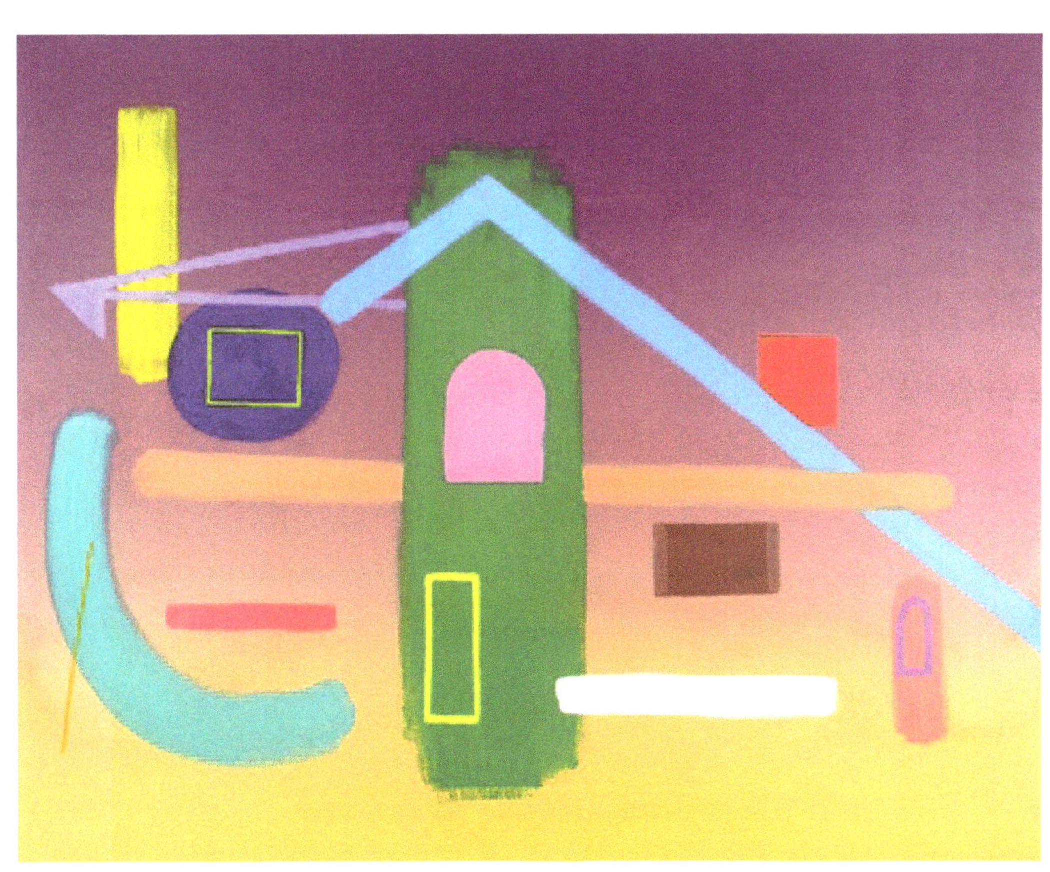

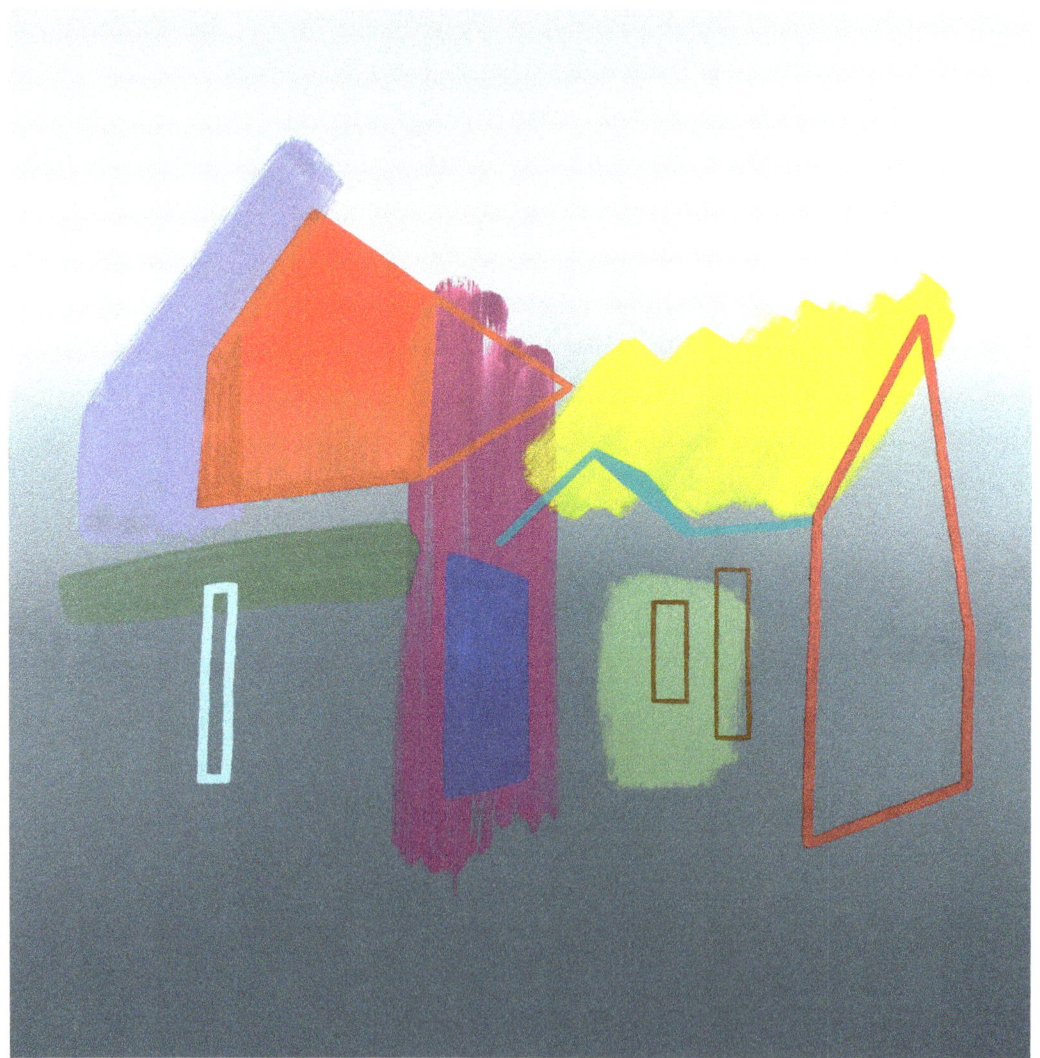

Floating in a sea of fog,

we're called home

by the glow of glistening rooftops

and slick window panes.

Yellow, a beacon of warmth,

and orange, a blaze of safety,

raise their voices through the white

and make their presence known.

Our vision shifts from soft to crisp

as we accept the invitation of shelter.

A cool blue retreat,

the offer of oasis

against a rising heat.

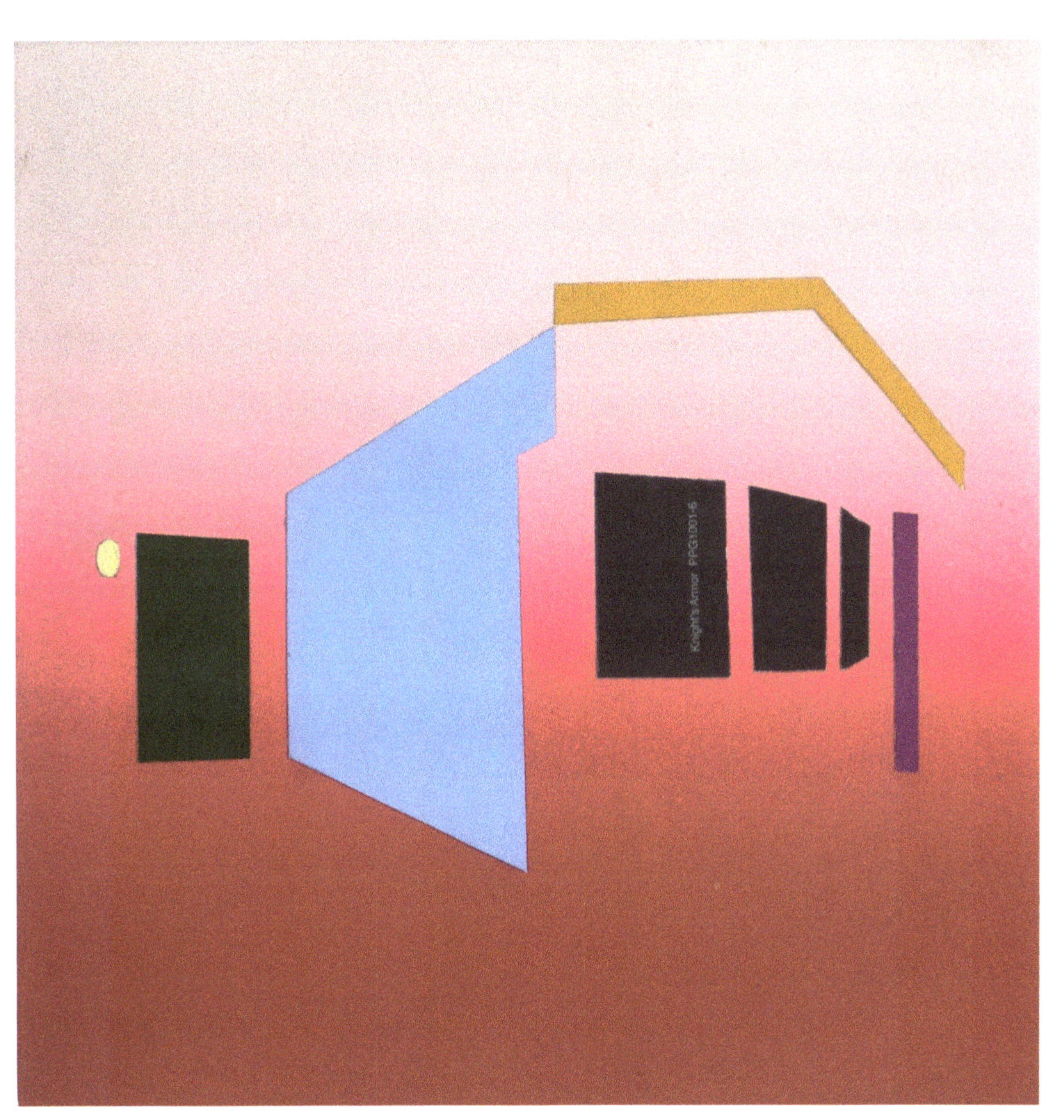
Knight's Armor PPG1001-6

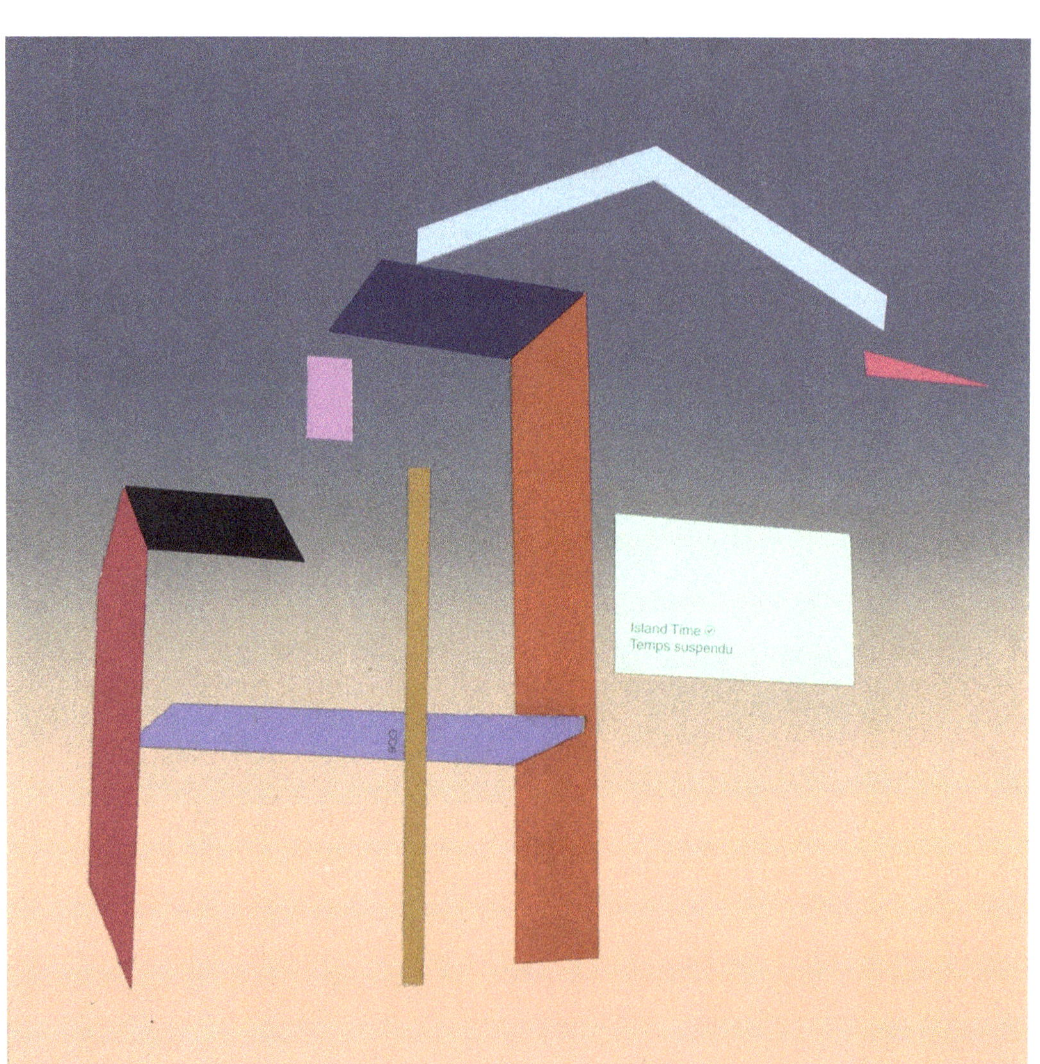

Island Time
Temps suspendu

I'll take my time

and leave nothing behind,

not a piece out of place

in this pick up sticks getaway.

Today blends smoothly into tomorrow

as I peek out the porthole

with a tall stemmed red

to toast the passing of the sun.

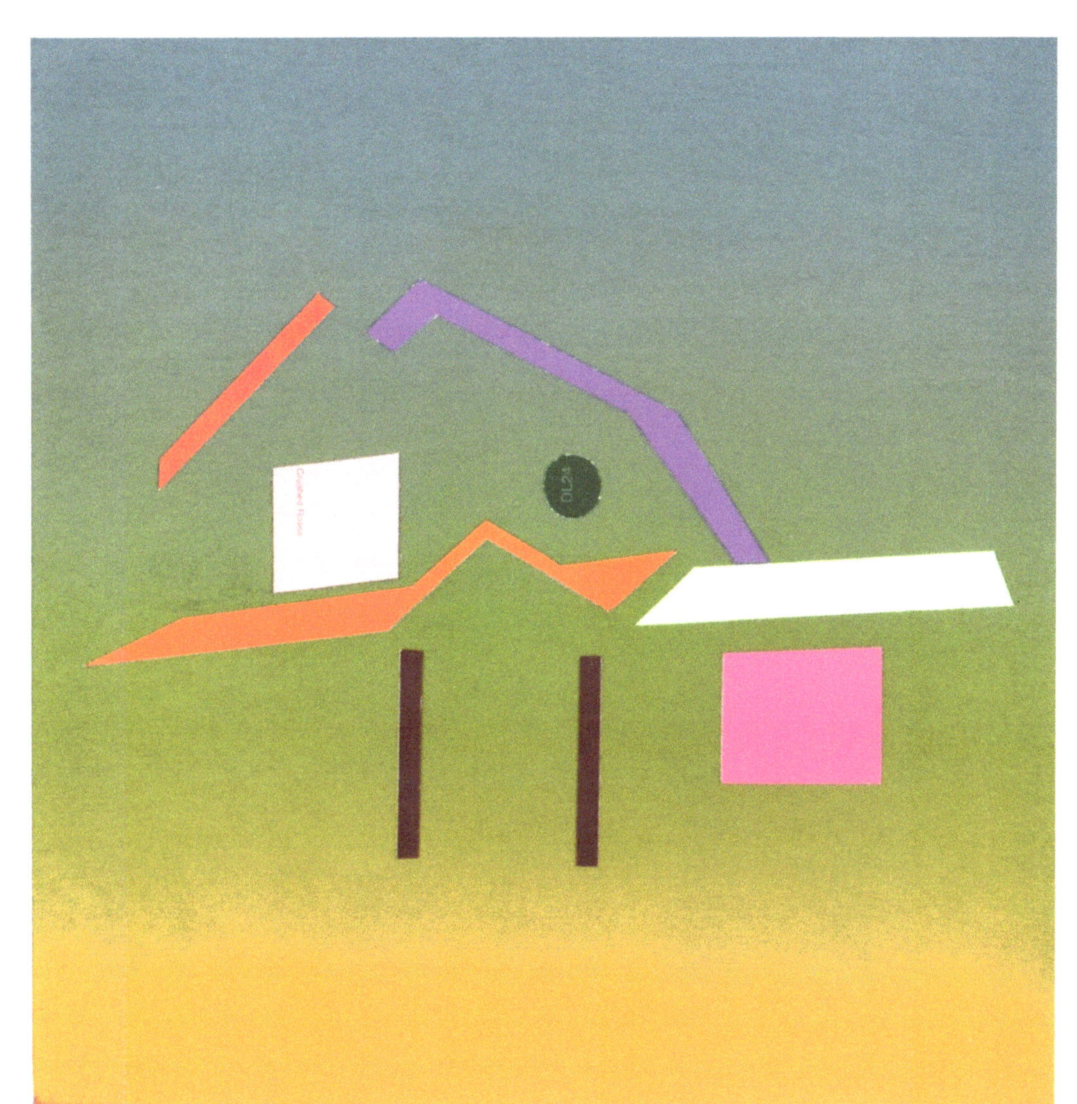
DL24

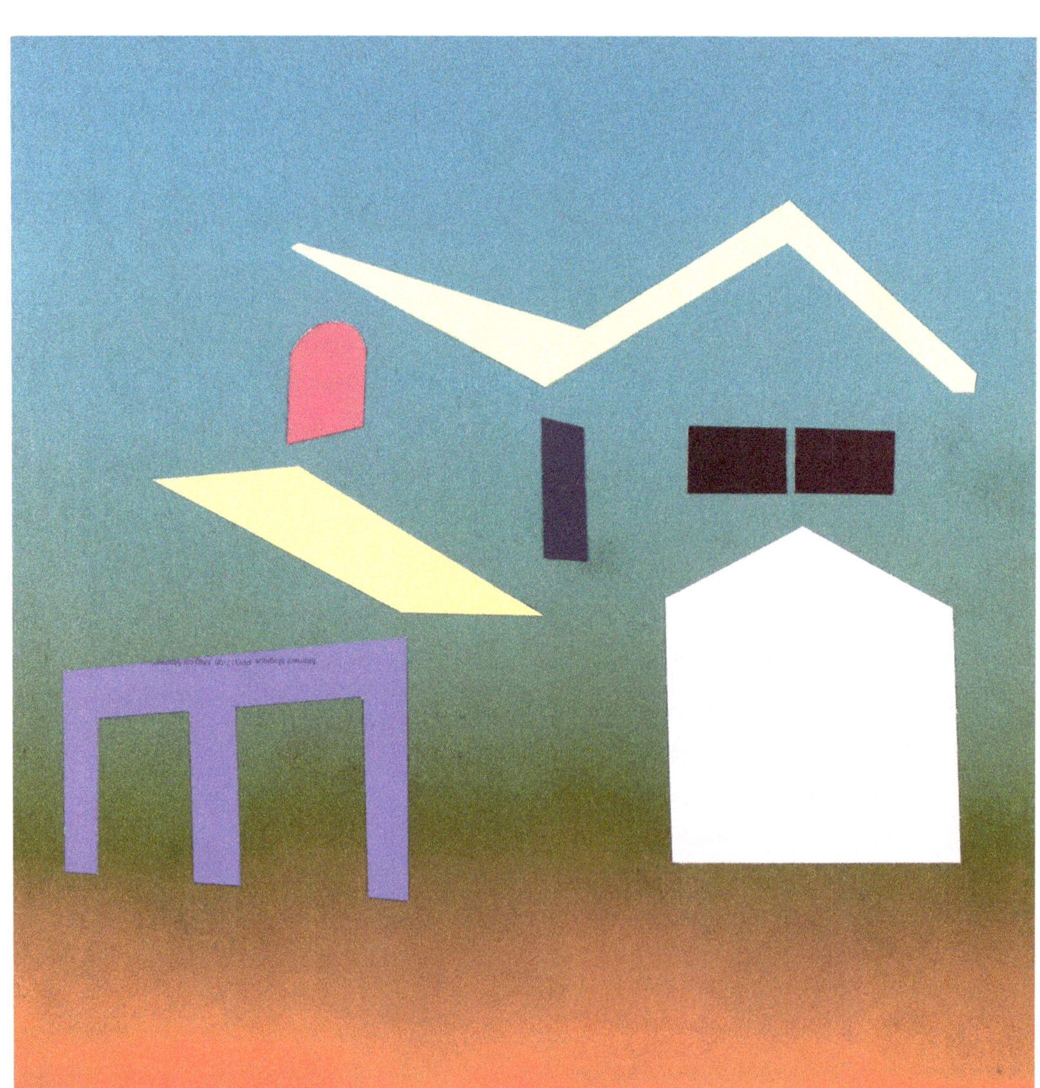

The day is broken by an orange glow.

It rises,

threatening to *wake my* bedroom *window*

and cast off the cool peace of sleep.

What a spot!

Perched on the edge of the world
and watching the sun leave the day,
the sky ebbs from gold to grey.

Sit on the stair and watch it fade away,
let the cool air wrap around you
and remind you why you let your roots
grow into this hard ground.

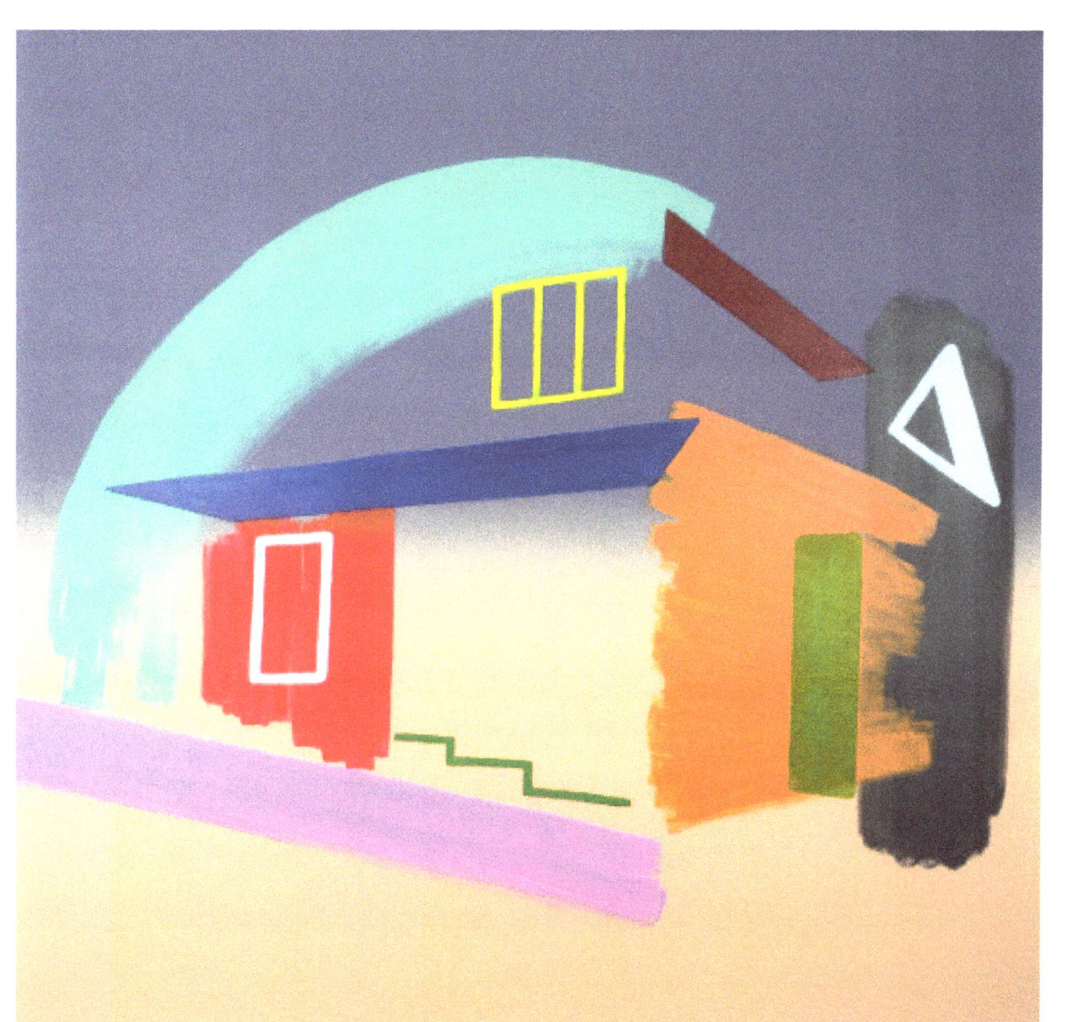

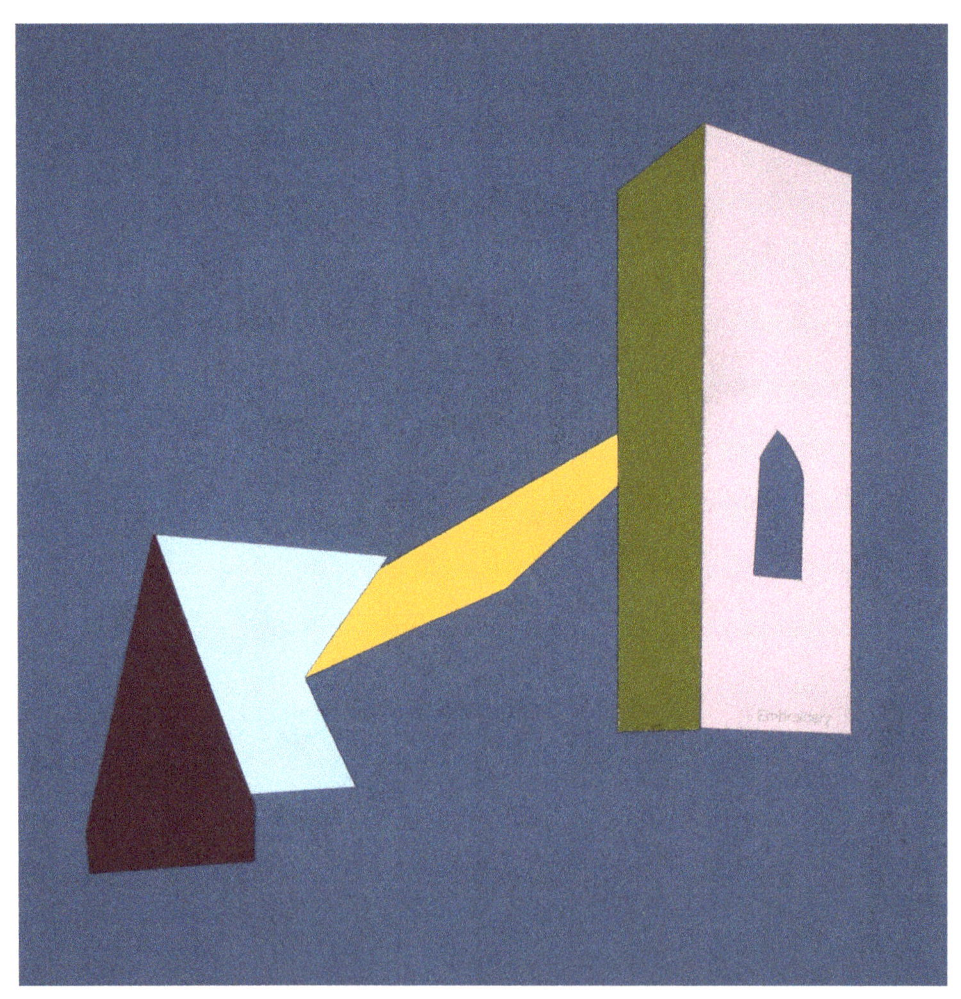

I stare my reflection in the face

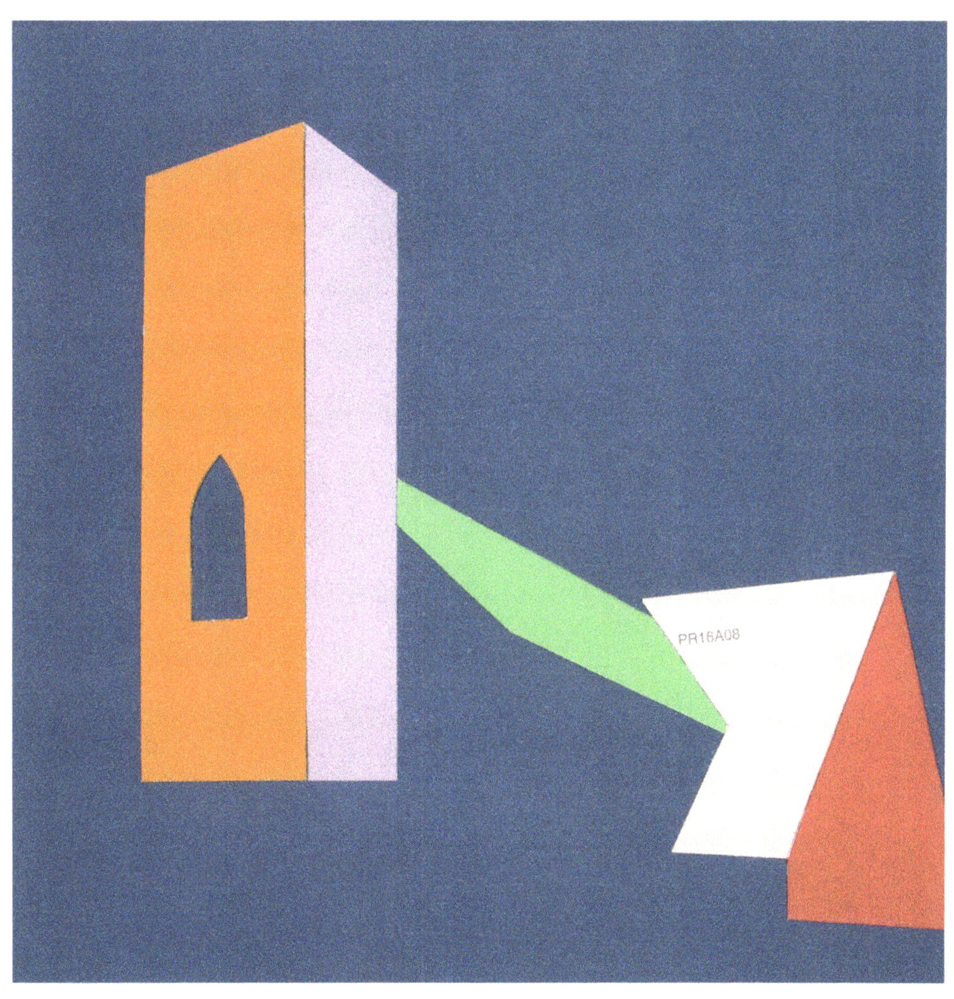

and ask her about the beyond

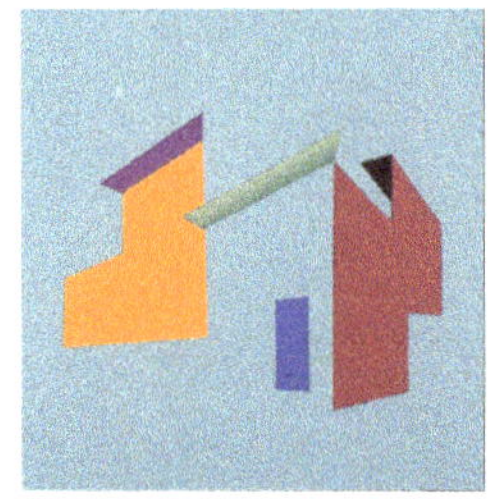

Dream Home # 5
8" x 8"
20.3 cm x 20.3 cm
paint chips & house paint
on panel
2019

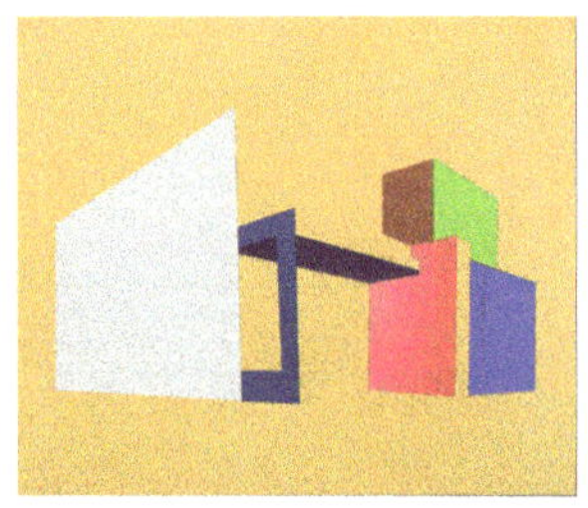

Dream Home # 6
10" x 12"
25.4 cm x 30.4 cm
paint chips & house paint
on panel
2019

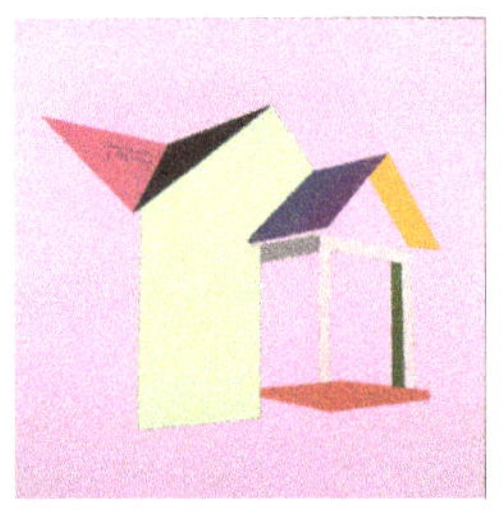

Dream Home # 8
10" x 10"
25.4 cm x 25.4 cm
paint chips & house paint
on panel
2019

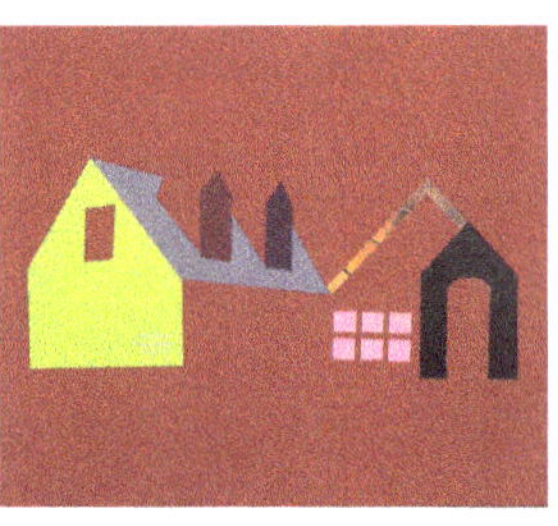

Dream Home # 11
10" x 12"
25.4 cm x 30.4 cm
paint chips & house paint
on panel
2019

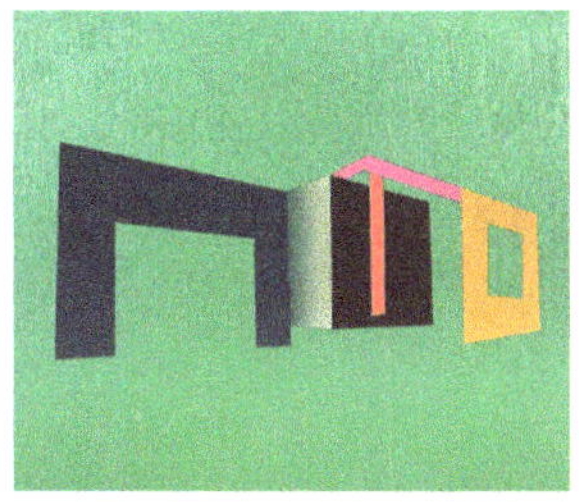

Dream Home # 13
10" x 12"
25.4 cm x 30.4 cm
paint chips & house paint
on panel
2019

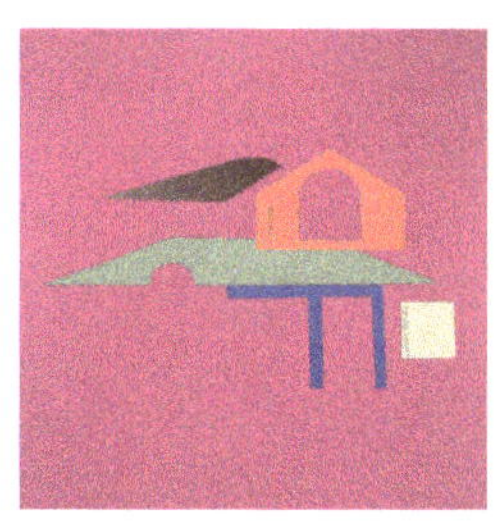

Dream Home # 15
8" x 8"
20.3 cm x 20.3 cm
paint chips & house paint
on panel
2019

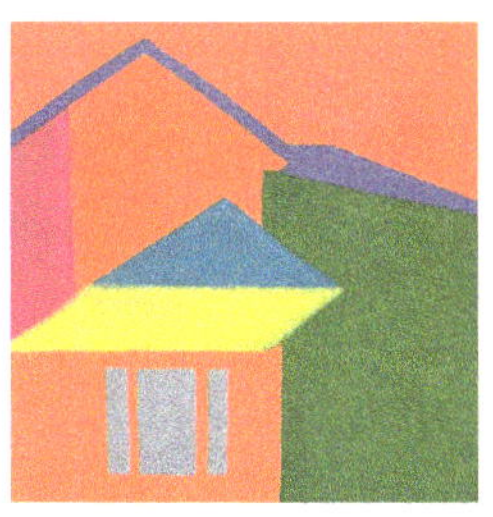

Dream Home # 16
16" x 16"
40.6 cm x 40.6 cm
oil & house paint on canvas
(on panel)
2019

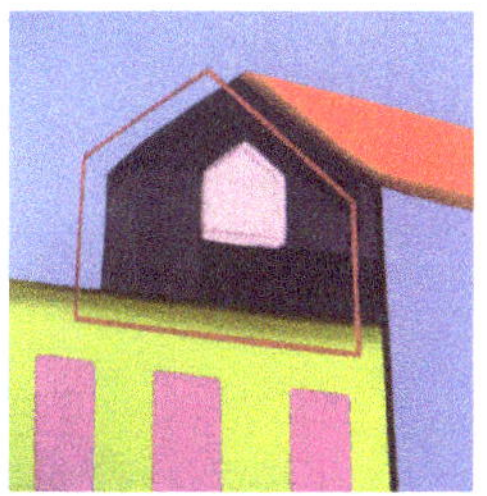

Dream Home # 18
20" x 20"
50.8 cm x 50.8 cm
oil & house paint on canvas
(on panel)
2019

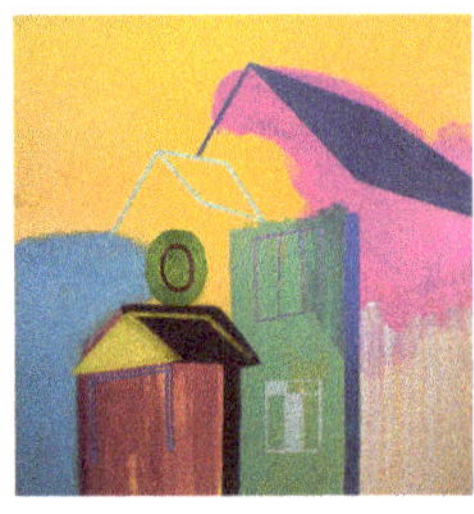

Dream Home # 19
36" x 36"
91.4 cm x 91.4 cm
house paint & oil paint
on panel
2019

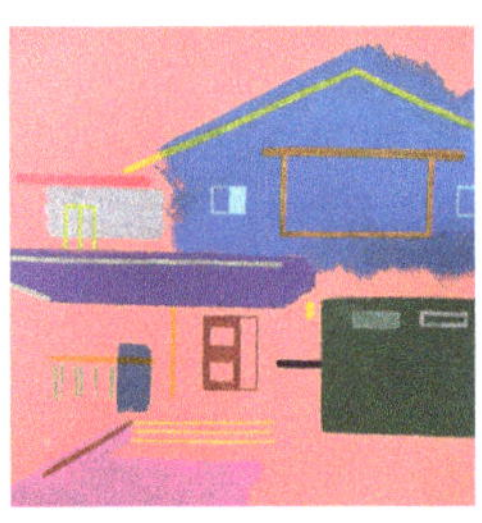

Dream Home # 21
48" x 48"
121.9 cm x 121.9 cm
house paint & oil paint
on panel
2019

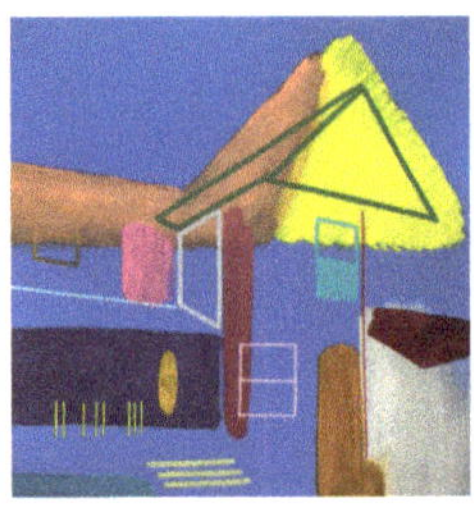

Dream Home # 22
48" x 48"
121.9 cm x 121.9 cm
house paint & oil paint
on panel
2019

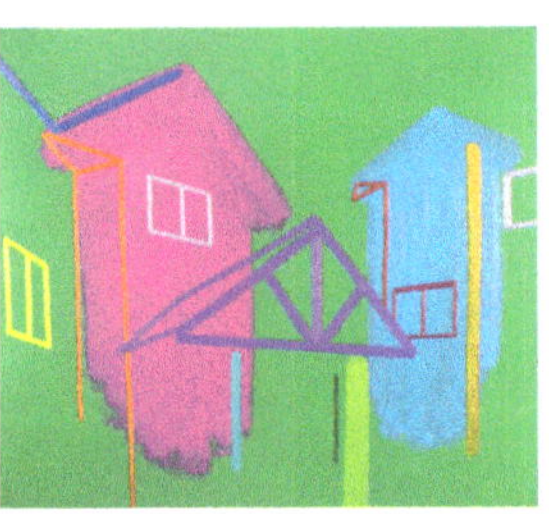

Dream Home # 24
36" x 42"
91.4 cm x 106.6 cm
house paint & oil paint
on panel
2019

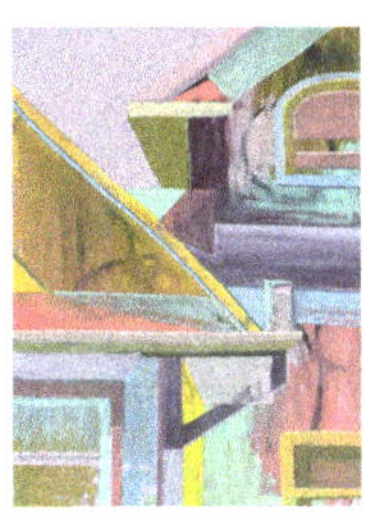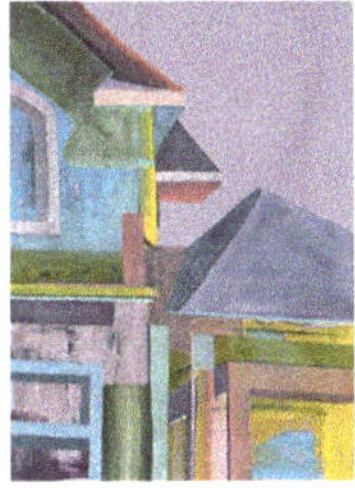

94 Tera Nova Drive, # 1,2 (each)
48" x 35 1/2"
121.9 cm x 90.2 cm
oil and house paint on canvas
2015

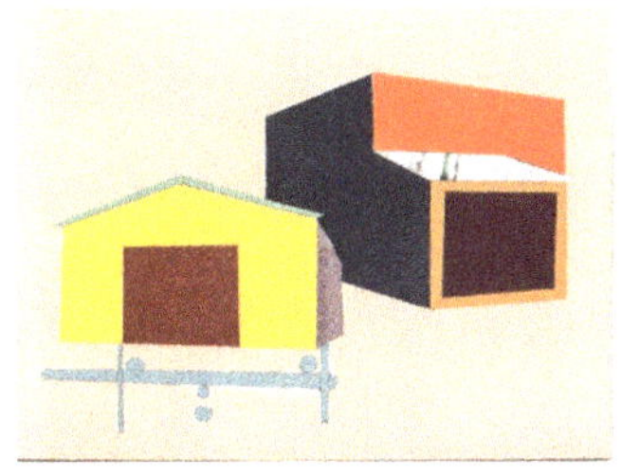

Little Heart's Ease
6" x 8"
15.2 cm x 20.3 cm
wood panel, house paint
& paper collage
2017

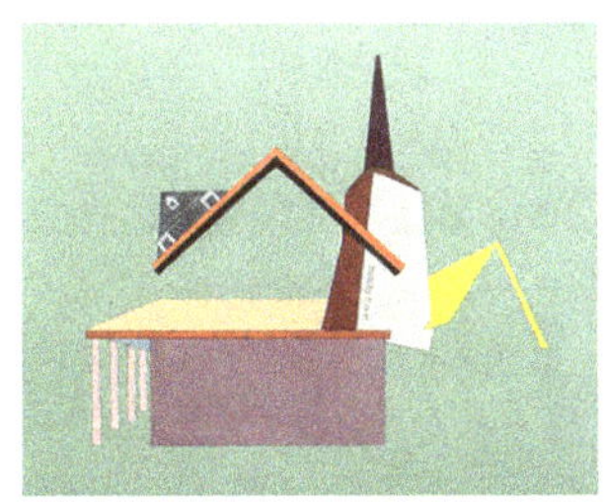

Beechy Cove
8" x 10"
20.3 cm x 25.4 cm
wood panel, house paint
& paper collage
2017

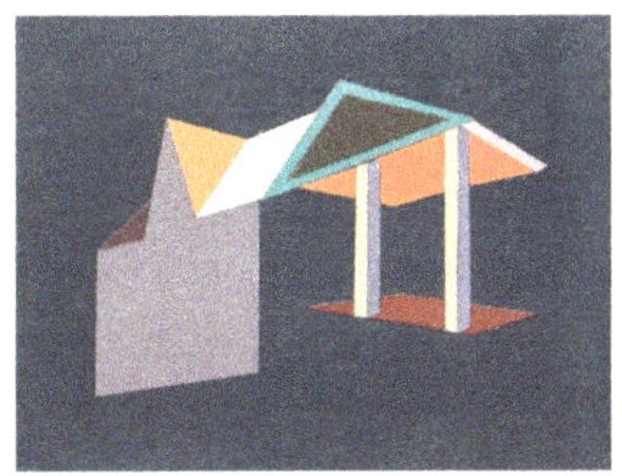

Duntara
6" x 8"
15.2 cm x 20.3 cm
wood panel, house paint
& paper collage
2017

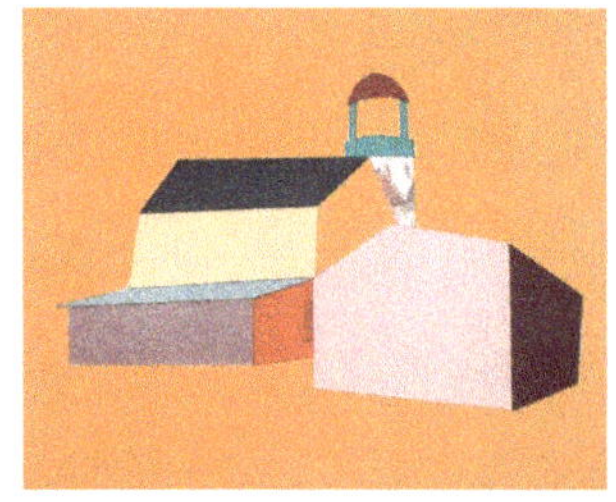

Red Ochre
8" x 10"
20.3 cm x 25.4 cm
wood panel, house paint
& paper collage
2017

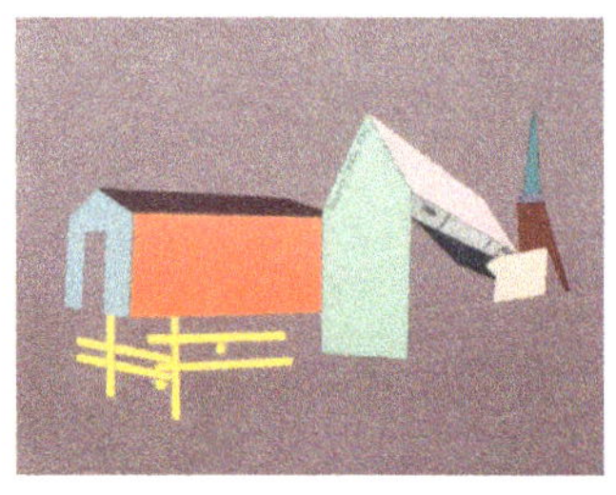

Sea Foam Green
6" x 8"
15.2 cm x 20.3 cm
wood panel, house paint
& paper collage
2017

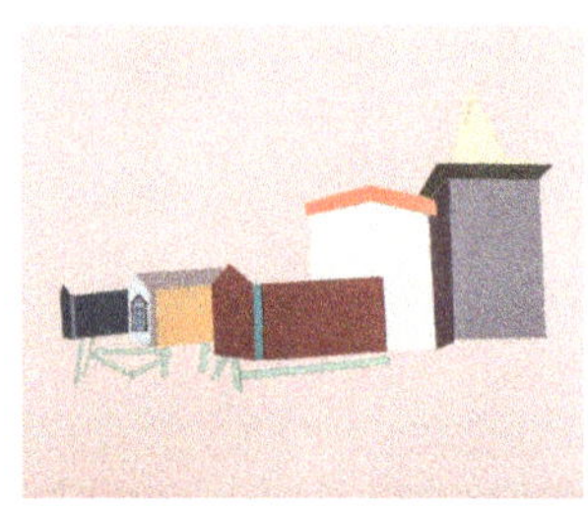

Maize
8" x 10"
20.3 cm x 25.4 cm
wood panel, house paint
& paper collage
2017

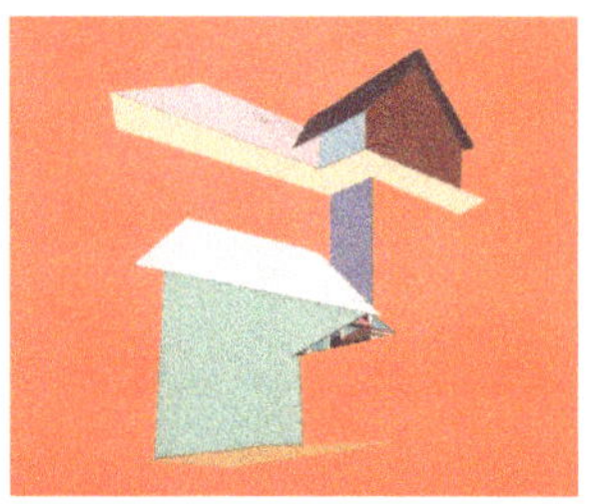

Cherry Pink
8" x 10"
20.3 cm x 25.4 cm
wood panel, house paint
& paper collage
2017

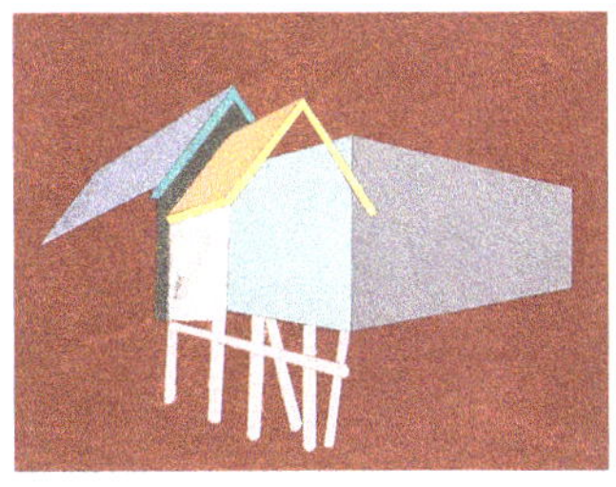

Bristol's Hope
6" x 8"
15.2 cm x 20.3 cm
wood panel, house paint
& paper collage
2017

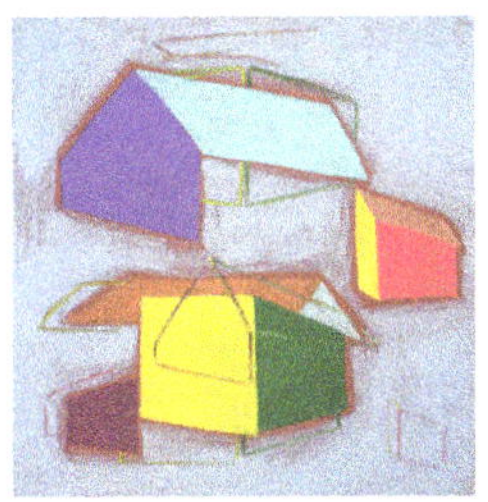

Ten Historic Towns # 1
36" x 36"
91.4 cm x 91.4 cm
oil & house paint
on panel
2018

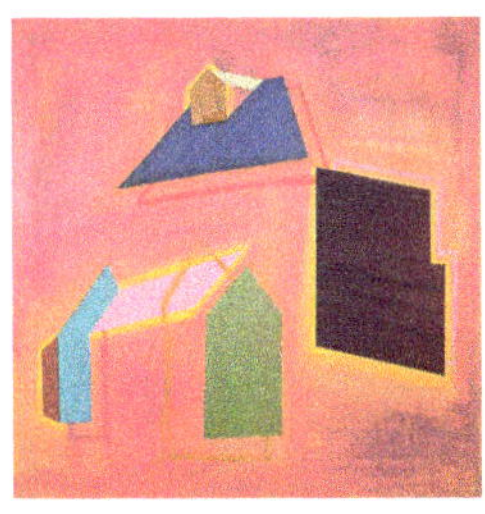

Ten Historic Towns # 2
36" x 36"
91.4 cm x 91.4 cm
oil & house paint
on panel
2019

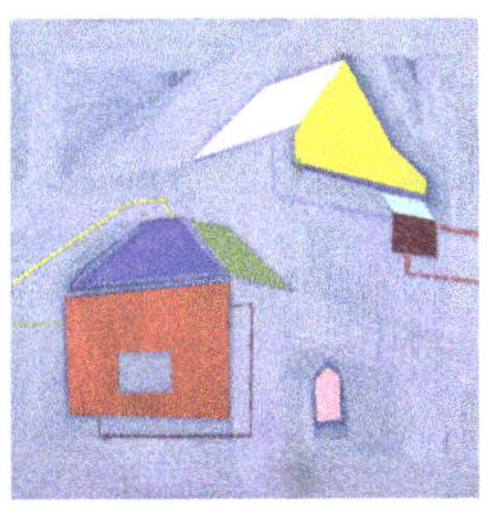

Ten Historic Towns # 3
16" x 16"
40.6 cm x 40.6 cm
oil & house paint
on panel
2019

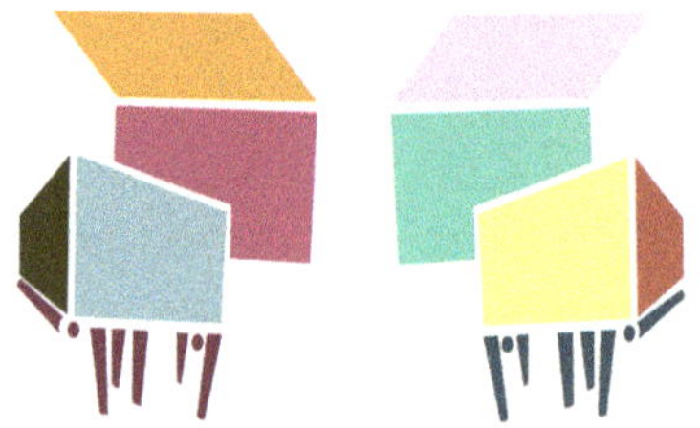 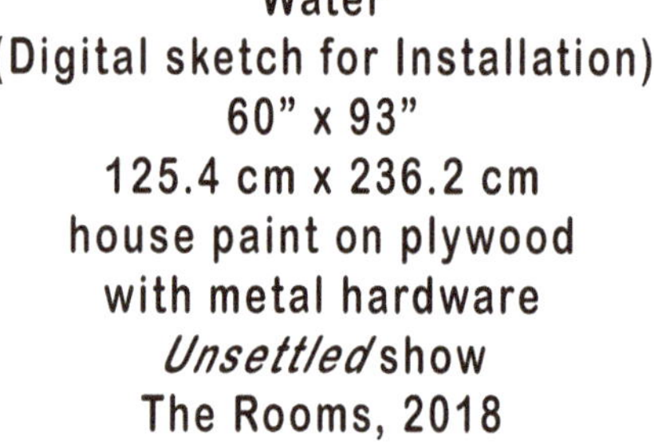

Water
(Digital sketch for Installation)
60" x 93"
125.4 cm x 236.2 cm
house paint on plywood
with metal hardware
Unsettled show
The Rooms, 2018

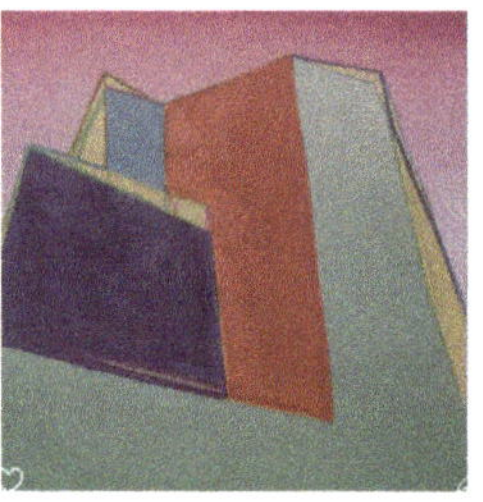

Steep Lines 1, # 2
48" x 48"
121.9 cm x 121.9 cm
oil & latex paint
on canvas
2017

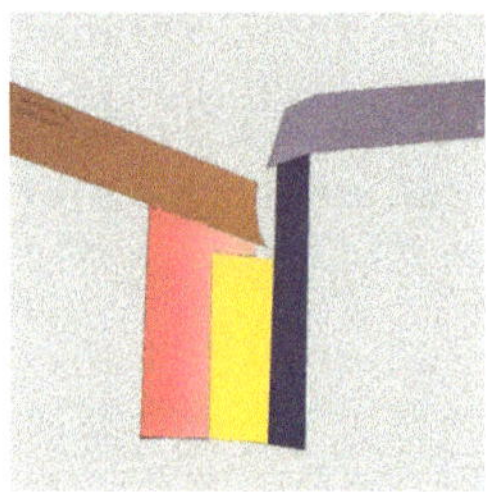

Steep Lines 2, # 5
8" x 8"
20.3 cm x 20.3 cm
paint chips, painted paper,
house paint on panel
2019

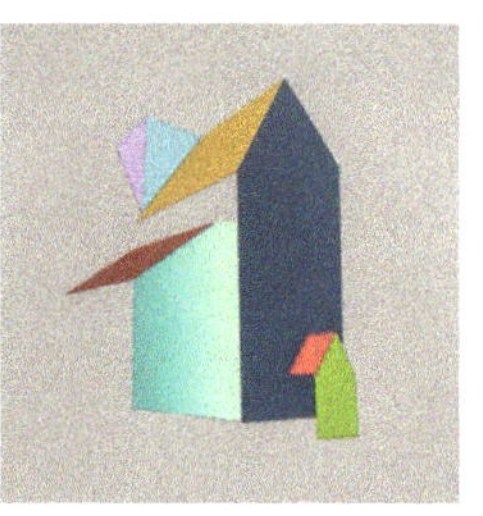

Steep Lines 2, # 6
8" x 8"
20.3 cm x 20.3 cm
paint chips, painted paper,
house paint on panel
2019

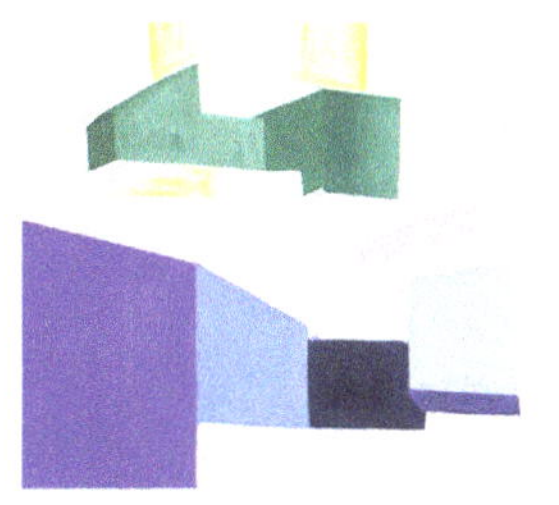

Almost Had It
48" x 60"
121.9 cm x 152.4 cm
oil & latex paint
on canvas
2016

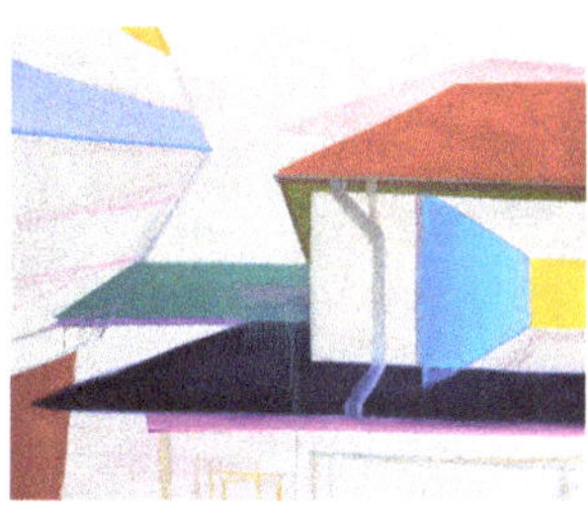

That's The Ticket
48" x 60"
121.9 cm x 152.4 cm
oil & latex paint
on canvas
2016

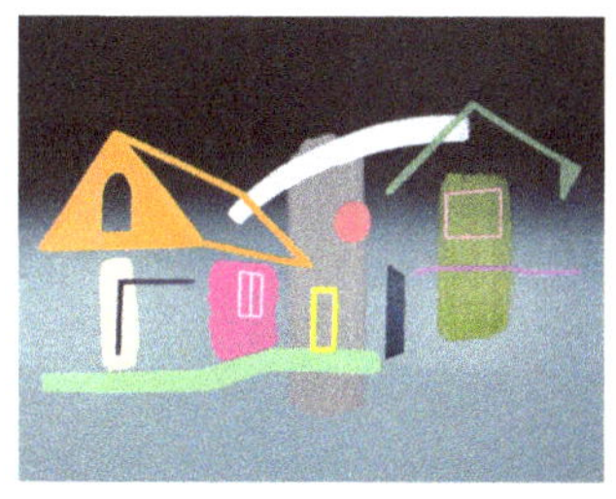

What A View # 1
30" x 24"
76.2 cm x 60.9 cm
oil & house paint
on panel
2020

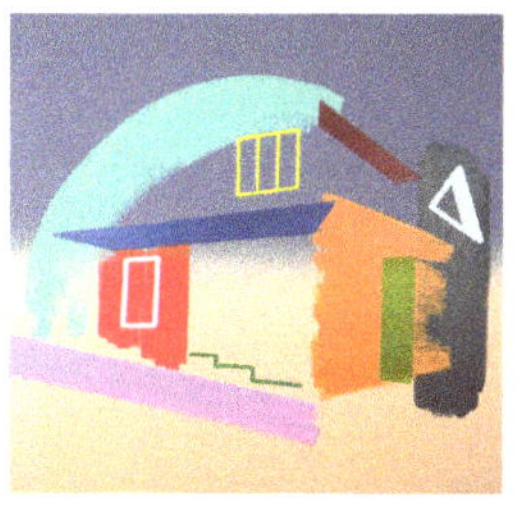

What A View # 3
30" x 30"
76.2 cm x 76.2 cm
oil & house paint
on panel
2020

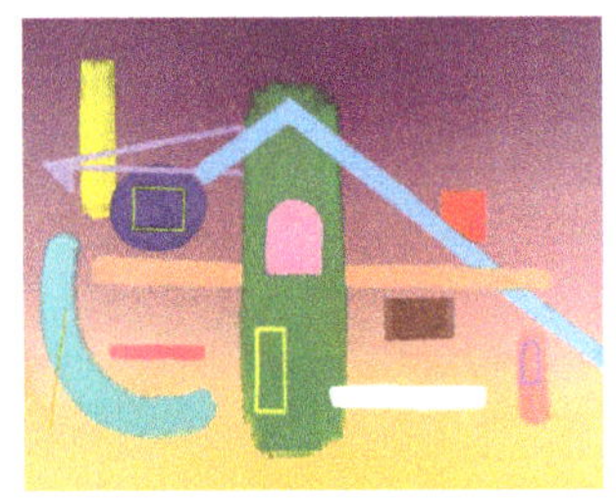

What a View # 4
30" x 34"
76.2 cm x 86.3 cm
oil & house paint
on panel
2020

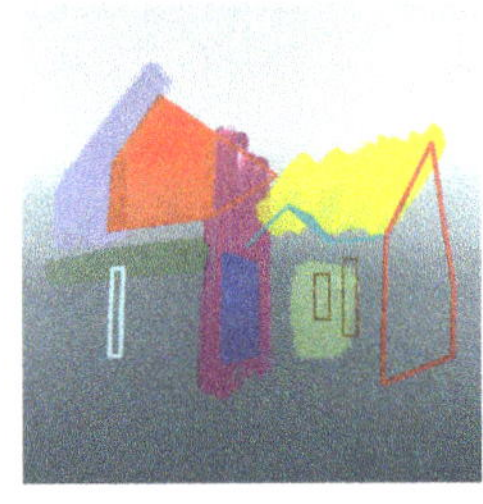

What a View # 5
30" x 30"
76.2 cm x 76.2 cm
oil & house paint
on panel
2020

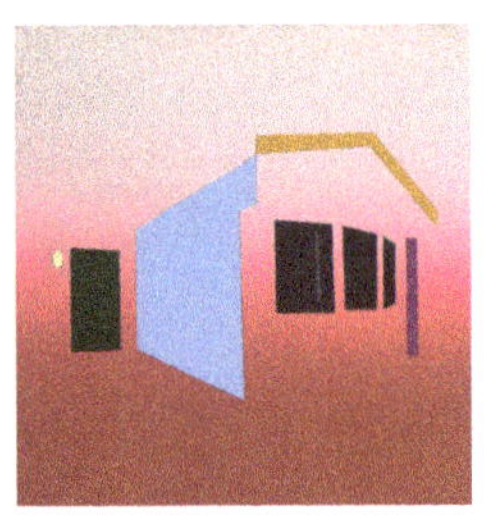

What a View # 7
8" x 8"
20.3 cm x 20.3 cm
wood panel, house paint &
paper collage
2020

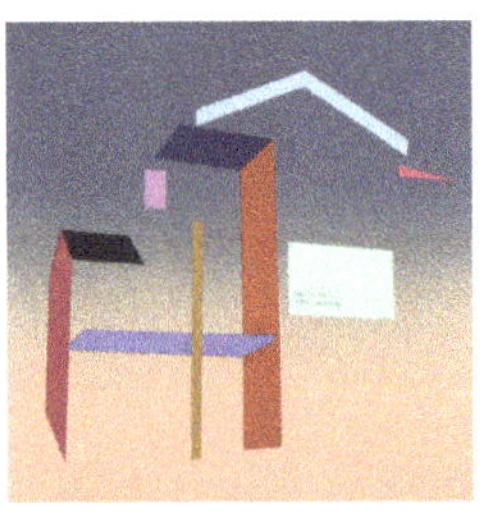

What a View # 8
10" x 10"
25.4 cm x 25.4 cm
wood panel, house paint &
paper collage
2020

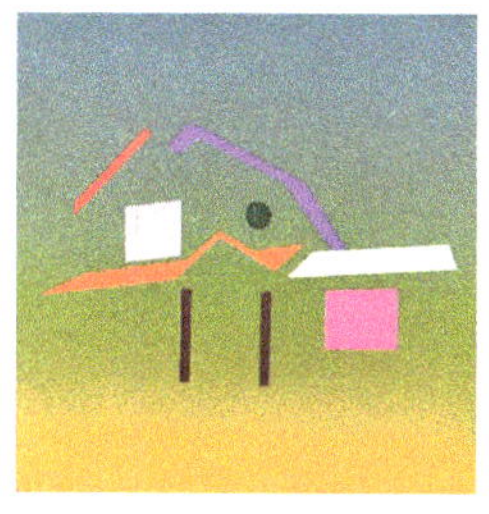

What a View # 9
10" x 10"
25.4 cm x 25.4 cm
wood panel, house paint &
paper collage
2020

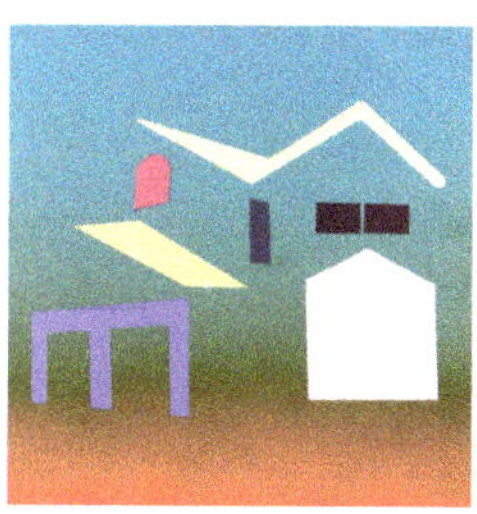

What a View # 10
12" x 12"
30 cm x 30 cm
wood panel, house paint &
paper collage
2020

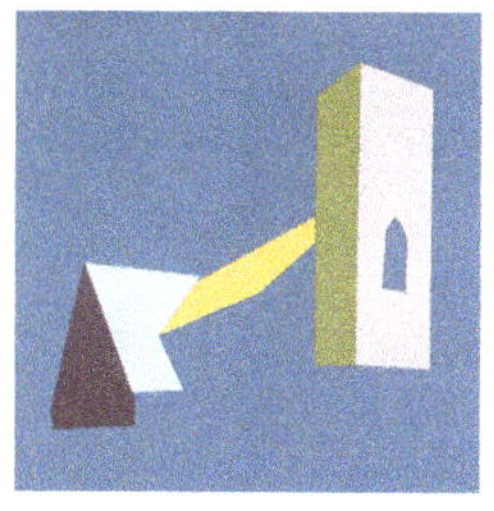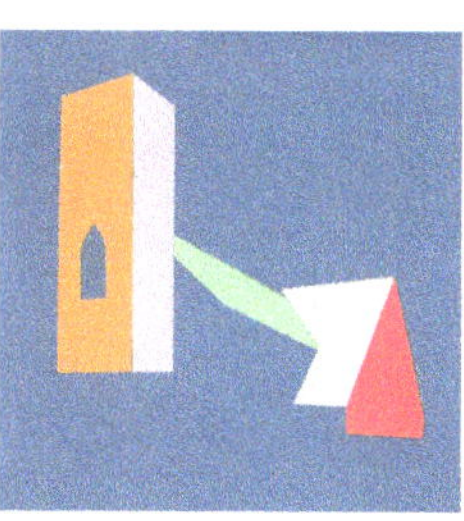

Earthly Eternal # 1
8" x 16"
20.3 cm x 40.6 cm
wood panel, house paint &
paper collage
2020

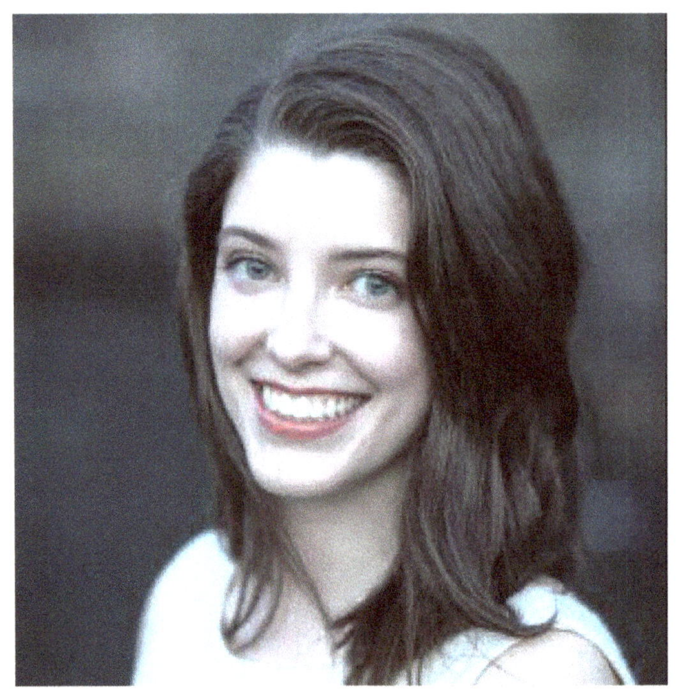

Artist Biography

Emily Pittman is a visual artist and writer based in St. John's, Newfoundland and Labrador. She earned an Honours BA (with Distinction), majoring in Studio Art and English from the University of Guelph. Emily is an instructor in the Art & Design Essentials program with the College of the North Atlantic and is represented by Christina Parker Gallery in St. John's, Newfoundland and Jones Gallery in St. John, New Brunswick. She was a finalist for Arts NL's 2019 Emerging Artist Award and has exhibited at venues including The Rooms Provincial art Gallery in St. John's, The Confederation Centre for the Arts in Charlottetown, Prince Edward Island , Eastern Edge Gallery in St. John's and the Boarding House Gallery in Guelph, Ontario. She has been featured on the cover of *Visual Arts News*, as well as in *Riddle Fence*, *The Overcast*, and *The St. John's Telegram*. Emily also co-founded *The Gathered Gallery* (*www.thegatheredgallery.com*).

For more detailed information, visit *www.emilypittman.ca*

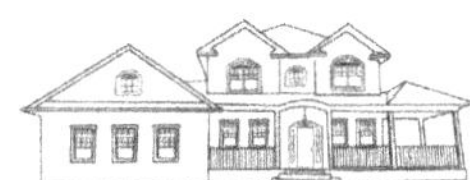

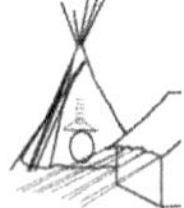